To Joe, Karen and Alison—
your support means everything to me.

FINANCIAL STATEMENT ANALYSIS

THE BASICS AND BEYOND

Year-End Data:		
Current assets	$145,090	$158.3
Current liabilities	42,000	76,2
	$ 7	$ 82.1
Working capital	725	6,7
	41,901	257,
Inventories	289,287	35,0
Pro	73,318	2,28
notes payable	2,268	
rrent debt		
Capital Invested:	$ 72,086	$ 27,3
Long-term debt	131,752	139,1
Stockholders' equity		

ROSE MARIE L. BUKICS

Library of Congress Cataloging in Publication Data Available

ISBN 1-55738-183-6

Printed in the United States of America

IPC

1 2 3 4 5 6 7 8 9 0

Acknowledgements

To Mary Murphy and Dick Johnston who read and reread the manuscript and offered invaluable comments. In addition, a special thanks to Dick Johnston for the writing on the price-earnings ratio in Chapter 7.

Financial Statements and Notes from the 1989 annual report provided courtesy of Mack Trucks, Inc., copyright 1990.

The following registered trademarks or service marks of Mack Trucks, Inc. and its subsidiaries appear in this book: Mack, Ultra-Liner, Super Liner, Mid-Liner, Bulldog, MFC, and MLS. TRUCS is a service mark of Shearson Lehman Hutton.

CONTENTS

CHAPTER 1

FINANCIAL STATEMENTS— AN OVERVIEW

Financial statements disclose the results of a company's business operations. The financial results represent the total of all financial transactions incurred over a period of time. Because financial statements are the output of the accounting system, they represent the mechanism used to summarize the many and often varied business activities.

Financial Statement Basics

The primary financial statements are those most often seen by the investor: The Balance Sheet, Statement of Income, Statement of Cash Flows, and the Statement of Changes in Stockholder's Equity. The most important concept governing preparation of these statements is an accounting principle known as "full disclosure." This principle requires that the financial statements provide all necessary and relevant information for an investor to make an informed investment decision. As a result, the primary financial statements identified above, coupled with the financial statement note disclosures, provide a foundation of information for investors.

The Balance Sheet discloses information on the company's financial position at a specific point in time. This statement lists the financial resources available for firm use (known in accounting terms as assets), and balances these resources with the financial obligations (liabilities) and ownership rights (shareholder's equity) within the organization. To illustrate, if a company's assets include a building used in their operations, it is possible that debt of some nature was incurred in acquiring such a resource. A corresponding examination of the liability section of the Balance Sheet, might identify an item such as a mortgage payable. Thus it would appear that the financing mechanism used to acquire the building was a mortgage agreement.

The Statement of Income, however, discloses the results of the company's operating activities over a specified period of time. This statement is a dynamic rather than a static statement. The contents of the Statement of Income provide information on the company's earning of income, as well as the corresponding expenses incurred in generating that income. It usually does not matter what the source of the income or expense is, i.e., primary operations or incidental transactions such as interest income. If the transaction occurred during the current time period, it will be reflected in the Statement of Income.

The Statement of Changes in Shareholder's Equity can be thought of as a link between the Statement of Income and the Balance Sheet. This statement explains the changes in the specific owner's equity accounts listed on the Balance Sheet. The change in the retained earnings account noted on the Balance Sheet is caused by the profit or loss for the current period, carried forward from the Statement of Income, and/or it can be affected by distribution of a dividend. Changes in the common or preferred stock accounts (including additional paid-in capital) are caused by additional contributions or permanent withdrawals of ownership interest.

The Statement of Cash Flows is the only statement prepared on a total cash basis. This statement was a new addition to the financial statement package in 1988 and replaces the former Statement of Changes in Financial Position. The Statement of Cash Flows summarizes the business activities and their corresponding impact on the cash position of the enterprise. It requires classifying cash generated or cash used in one of three ways: operating, investing or financing activities. In addition, the Statement of Cash Flows is a link to the Balance Sheet since the cash balances reflected on the Statement of Cash Flows must match the cash balances listed on the current Balance Sheet.

A published set of financial statements is provided in Appendix 1 for reference purposes. In Appendix 2, the relationships between the financial statements are illustrated. Reference to these appendices will aid the reader as each of the financial statements are discussed in greater detail in Chapters 2 through 4. One additional item must be noted when discussing financial statements. Often, a set of financial statements will be prefaced with the word "consolidated," i.e., Consolidated Balance Sheet, Consolidated Statement of Income etc.. This simply means that the information presented represents the sum of all activities of both the parent company and any operating subsidiaries.

Supplemental Disclosures

One may question the level of detail contained in the financial statements. Published financial's, such as those available to the investor, do not contain a significant level of detail compared to those used by operating managers. However, additional details are normally disclosed in the supplemental information accompanying the financial statements. The use of the financial statements, combined with the supplemental disclosures, provide a basis for making intelligent investing decisions.

Need for a Summarization Process

Financial statement information is the end product of a somewhat lengthy accounting process, and represents the sum of all financial transactions. The financial transaction which initiated the need for an accounting entry began as an individual event, recorded at the cost incurred at the time of the transaction. As the processing of this transaction continues, it proceeds through various summarization stages in the accounting cycle and is grouped with transactions of a similar nature. As a result, it becomes only one part, no longer specifically identifiable, of a much larger data base. Without such a summarization, it would be difficult, if not impossible, to make sense out of the large volume of financial activity that occurs.

For example, in the earlier discussion, the acquisition of a building was reflected as a resource of the company and the financial obligation was easily identifiable as a mortgage payable. However, that transaction was simplified. In fact, the company may have acquired several buildings, using a variety of financing techniques, including a down payment, short-term borrowing, a mortgage agreement or even a lease. Only a careful reading of the Balance Sheet, in conjunction with the financial statement note disclosures, would indicate some level of detail concerning such a transaction.

Inherent in this summarization process are some practical constraints. Information provided to the investor is in summary form with minimal detail. Thus, financial statement data alone may not provide enough information for an investment decision. An additional constraint of the summarization process is the form of the financial statements. Because of accounting regulations governing financial statement preparation, the form of the transaction, rather than its substance, might be emphasized in the attempt to provide comparable financial statement data. This attempt at financial statement standardization may be incompatible with the objectives of an investor. A further consideration is that the summarization of similar financial events assumes that all transactions "fit" into a categorical description. It is safe to assume that this is not always the case.

Although there are problems inherent in such a summarization process, it is important to remember that in order to process large volumes of financial data in an efficient, logical and systematic manner, some mechanism for summarization must be used. In each of the following chapters the limitations of the accounting and reporting mechanisms used, as well as their impact on financial statement data, are discussed in greater detail.

The key word in discussing business transactions and financial statements, is "financial." There are business transactions that occur that do not have immediate financial implications. Therefore, these transactions will not be reflected in the primary financial statements. However, if the impact of these non-financial transactions is potentially significant, the company must disclose such a transaction in the supplemental information. Again, it must be stressed that it is important for investors to read the financial statements, in conjunction with the supplemental disclosures accompanying such statements, to grasp a thorough understanding of the company's financial activity.

How Are Financial Statements Used?

Financial statements are read and analyzed by a wide variety of users. Bankers, stock market analysts, creditors, investors and employees read the published financial statements. However, the information obtained from the statements is used differently depending upon the focus of the reader.

A primary consumer of financial statement data is the individual investor. An investor reads and analyzes financial statements to gather relevant information on a potential or existing investment. That information is then used to determine the investment caliber of a stock and to identify yield and growth opportunities. This involves assessing both risk and return potential.

The specific data provided in the primary financial statements, coupled with the accompanying disclosures, provides a useful data base. In addition, the investor can acquire information from many of the readily available investment publications, for example, Value Line Investment Survey published by Bernhard in New York. Financial statement analysis, often facilitated by such publications, form a basis for determining the risk and return potential of an investment decision.

Because the financial statements represent management's statement about the company's operating results, they become the vehicle used to inform those outside of the company. It is safe to say that the financial statements form the critical data base from which many investors are making investment decisions. As a result, it is important to understand how financial statements are prepared and the limitations inherent in accounting data.

How Are Financial Statements Prepared?

Many financial statement readers do not have a background in finance or accounting. However, with some basic understanding on how and when financial statements are prepared, it becomes easier to comprehend, analyze and utilize the data contained in the statements.

Financial statements are normally prepared by a financial accounting/reporting group within the company. The source of the information prepared by the group, and summarized in the financial statements, comes from the accounting system. The information is entered into the accounting system as a function of data entry in each of the operating departments.

The responsibility for the financial statement information lies with the management of the company. Even in year-end statements, when an audit opinion has been rendered, it is management, not the outside accounting firm, who has responsibility for the financial statement contents.

Financial statement preparation and presentation is fairly standardized. The presentation format is dictated by either the Securities and Exchange Commission (SEC) for those reports filed with the governmental regulatory agency, or by the accounting industry standard setting body, known as the Financial Accounting Standards Board (FASB), or by other industry-specific regulatory agencies. That is not to say that financial statement presentation is completely standardized. Judgement in applying accounting principles, as well as reporting alternatives must still be exercised.

It is important to make a distinction between the application of accounting principles that govern the determination of the financial statement elements and those that govern the financial reporting of such events. Both of these areas allow for the exercise of judgement. For example, when determining the method of depreciation to be used in recording the utilization of plant and equipment, there are several alternative, yet acceptable, methods which can be selected.

Straight-line depreciation is a uniform write-off of dollars over the life of the equipment. An accelerated method of depreciation, such as double declining balance, records varying dollars for depreciation in each year of the asset life. To illustrate, acquiring equipment for $10,000 with expected use of 5 years and no salvage value, would cause depreciation of $2000 in year one of the asset life (and in each subsequent year) under straight-line depreciation, but double declining balance would show $4000 in year 1.

Both of the depreciation methods referred to above are acceptable under generally accepted accounting principles, yet they affect the book value (cost less accumulated depreciation) of the equipment shown on the Balance Sheet, $8000 under straight-line depreciation and $6000 under double declining balance, at the end of year 1. In addition, the dollars recorded for annual depreciation expense on the Statement of Income would be different. Thus the exercise of judgement in selecting a depreciation method, causes a difference in the financial statement elements, i.e., the asset value reported in the Balance Sheet and the current period depreciation expense on the Statement of Income.

It is important to note that companies actually have two decision to make regarding depreciation—which method to use for tax depreciation and which method to use for recording depreciation in the financial accounting records (known as book depreciation). It is the latter that is reflected in the published financial statements, and it is not required that book and tax depreciation methods be one and the same. It is advisable for a company to choose an accelerated method of depreciation for tax purposes (tax law governs the calculation of such accelerated depreciation). Higher depreciation write-offs lead to lower reported profits which in turn leads to reduced taxes. However, for financial statement purposes, many companies choose straight-line since accelerated depreciation causes a reduction in the reported profits of the enterprise with no offsetting benefits in the financial records.

What does this mean to an investor? Only that there should be recognition of the differences in depreciation methods and the resulting asset value assigned to plant and equipment is dependant upon such depreciation methodology. Depreciation and its corresponding book value does not ensure a realistic value of the asset in terms of current market or replacement value of that asset.

Choices concerning financial statement presentation can also be made. Acquisition of common stock of another company is recorded at the cost of the acquisition. The classification of such an investment on the Balance Sheet requires the exercise of judgement. The security itself has no maturity and may or may not be liquid. Where should the investment be shown in the Balance Sheet? There are two possible places, as a short-term/ current asset located with the cash of the company or as a long-term investment. The major distinction between these two locations is based on time. Yet, the security itself is an open-ended investment. As a result, it is usually the discretion of management, based on their intent when purchasing the security, which determines where such an investment is presented on the Balance Sheet.

Another item to consider when evaluating financial statement presentation is the impact of industry peculiarities. The basics for financial statement presentation are altered if the company is in certain industries, such as the utility or insurance industry. For example, a company's financial resources are usually listed in the order of liquidity, i.e., how fast the asset can be converted to cash. In the utility industry, however, the first resources listed are property, plant and equipment. Although this appears to be a deviation from the normal presentation, it is required by the Federal Energy Regulatory Agency (FERC) and is considered standard industry practice. Information on industry standards governing financial reporting can be found in the summary of significant accounting policies in the notes to the financial statements.

When Are Financial Statements Prepared?

Financial statements are normally prepared by businesses on a monthly basis. Operating and financial managers use these reports as an aid in managing the business. However, these monthly statements are normally not available to individuals or groups outside the business.

Quarterly financial statements are published by the organization and are designed to provide those outside of the company with information on an on-going basis. Quarterly data represents the sum of the operating activity for the prior 3 months and is also subject to SEC, FASB and other regulatory agency accounting and reporting regulations. Most large companies prepare their quarterly data (and monthly data for operating managers) on the same basis as the information prepared at year end. Although they do not actually "close the books" other than at year-end, the use of monthly and quarterly worksheets accomplishes the same objective. As a result, quarterly data, summed for the year, will equal the data disclosed in the year-end annual report.

Quarterly data is not significantly different in context or presentation than the data found in the annual year-end reports, with one major exception. Year-end data most likely is audited, i.e., evaluated by an outside third party who objectively determines that the results stated by the company are reasonable.

What are the implications of this for an investor? Simply, that data contained in an audited annual report is more reliable because it has an objective opinion as to its reasonableness. That is not to say that quarterly data is unreliable. As a timely measure of the on-going business activity, quarterly data usually provides useful information. Another difference between quarterly and year-end data is the level of detail. Normally more information is provided in the year-end annual report. If an investor wants to make an intelligent investment decision, the more information available, the more likely a wise decision will result. Before considering an investment, it is imperative that annual year-end reports be evaluated.

Financial Statement Disclosure

It is fairly common to think of financial statement information as the numbers shown in each of the financial statements. However, there is additional data investors need to know that does not lend itself to a "dollars and cents" presentation. This additional information is usually provided in the financial statement disclosures, most commonly called "notes."

Note disclosures are the narrative explanations that accompany published financial statements. (See Appendix 1 for an illustration of note disclosures.) They provide information on transactions that cannot be reduced to a number in a financial statement. Note disclosures also provide "behind the scenes" information which supplements the condensed format of the financial statements. The note disclosures contain a wealth of information that needs to be thoroughly understood by the investor before making an investment decision.

Some of the note disclosures take the form of supplemental schedules. These provide a listing of the numerical components of a number presented in total in the financial statements. These schedules facilitate the presentation of what is often complex financial data. Due to the importance of note disclosures, an entire chapter of this book has been dedicated to the topic. (See Chapter 6)

Other Financial Information

In addition to the financial statements and the accompanying notes, investors need to understand other information that normally is considered part of the financial statement "package."

The year-end financial statements and notes are often part of an "annual report" published by a company. Contained in the annual report is a host of information, some portions of which are more critical to the investor than others. It is often a colorful, well produced package that needs to be read carefully. Enclosed in the annual report is typically a letter/discussion from the chairman to the stockholders, an operating review summary, selected financial highlights, a narrative on the company and its environment, a financial review, shareholder information, and a listing of the directors and officers. Other components may also be included at the discretion of the company.

The financial statement information and note disclosures are usually in the financial review section. This section also includes management's discussion and analysis, a statement of management's responsibility for financial reporting, and the auditor's report or "opinion."

The auditor's opinion gives a statement as to the reasonableness or fairness of the financial information presented by the company's management. It is often required by a regulatory agency or outside creditor, and its purpose is to provide an objective statement about the company's operating results and financial position. This is an important part of the annual report package from an investor's perspective.

If the report is an unqualified opinion, known in accounting jargon as a "clean" opinion, this should provide the investor with a level of assurance as to the company's financial results. If the opinion is qualified, adverse or a disclaimer, this should cause an investor to thoroughly check on the nature of the transaction that caused such an opinion to be issued.

Managements Discussion and Analysis

The section in the annual report called "Management's Discussion and Analysis," is required by the Securities and Exchange Commission. In fact, this is an area which has received attention in recent times. In May of 1989, the SEC issued an interpretive release clarifying the nature and content of the MD&A.

MD&A is a discussion that should provide investors with management's perspective or viewpoint on the results of the operating activities. Specifically, it requires discussion on the company's liquidity, capital requirement's and results of operations. It also requires discussion of any demands or trends with significant or material impact on the company's present or continuing operations. This interpretive release does not represent new requirements, but is a clarifying statement as to the specific nature of the MD&A contents.

Financial Statement Details

Most of the discussion in this chapter has focused on general financial statement information. The logical point of discussion now moves from the general to the specific, beginning with the Balance Sheet in Chapter 2.

THE BALANCE SHEET

The Balance Sheet is a statement of a company's financial resources (assets), financial obligations (liabilities) and ownership interest (shareholder's equity.) Another name for the Balance Sheet currently gaining favor as a more descriptive title is the Statement of Financial Position or the Statement of Financial Condition.

Balance Sheet Basics

The Balance Sheet (see Appendix 1) provides a list of a firm's resources and indicates whether such resources were obtained from incurring a financial obligation or from capital contributions. That is why a Balance Sheet "balances." Funds had to be used to acquire the resources, and a firm can only acquire those funds from three sources: (1) borrowing, (2) ownership contributions (contributed capital), and (3) earnings retained in the business (earned capital.)

Borrowing can come from a variety of creditors such as suppliers, banks, or bond holders. Increases in capital can come from two primary sources, additional contributions by shareholders, and the retained earnings from the company's operations.

The Balance Sheet information provides an overall view of the firm's financial position at a specific point in time. In essence, it shows what assets the firm has and who has claim on those assets.

Although the Balance Sheet lists the account balances of resources and obligations and ownership that are the result of all business activities, it does not provide information on how or when those transactions occurred. The financial transaction flow that causes changes in Balance Sheet accounts are reflected on The Statement of Income and the Statement of Changes in Shareholder Equity. Thus, changes in each of those two statements cause corresponding changes in various accounts on the Balance Sheet. Simply stated, there are few financial transactions that do not have Balance Sheet implications.

How and When Is a Balance Sheet Prepared?

A Balance Sheet is normally dated the last day of the accounting period, whether the reporting period is monthly, quarterly or annually. That is not to say that the actual preparation is on the last day. In fact, it is usually several days past the last day of the cycle before all financial information can be processed. Therefore, a Balance Sheet dated on December 31, 1990 was probably prepared in January 1991. But the balances reflected in the account totals are those as of the last day of the year. Practical constraints make this process a necessity.

A Balance Sheet is often prepared monthly for the company's operating and financial managers. Publication of the Balance Sheet to those outside the company usually takes place at quarter-end or year-end when overall disclosure of the company's finances occurs. In the published Balance Sheet, attention to proper presentation and format is essential. That is not to say that all Balance Sheets will be identical, but some level of uniformity is desirable in order to facilitate comparability and interpretation.

Balance Sheet format and presentation can take one of two forms. The account format (as shown in Appendix 1) lists the assets on one side, balanced by the liabilities and equity shown on the opposing column or page. The report format lists the assets, with the liabilities shown directly underneath, subsequently followed by the equity accounts. Each of these formats are presently used. The actual disclosure of information within these two presentation formats is dictated by generally accepted accounting principles and industry standards.

How Does an Investor Use Balance Sheet Information?

An investor will usually have questions concerning a company's financial condition, specifically their financial structure and commitments. Examination of the Balance Sheet will in many instances provide answers to such questions if the investor knows where to look. An investor assessment is often facilitated by performing financial statement analysis, often ratio analysis, on the financial statements. Ratio and financial statement analysis will be explored in depth in Chapter 7.

Key information on the Balance Sheet, combined with the detailed information found in the notes to the financial statements (see Chapter 6 for additional information on note disclosures), provides answers to the questions often asked by investors. Such questions are as follows:

(1)   What types of assets does the company own?
(2)   Where and how did they obtain the necessary funds to acquire such assets?
(3)   What are the restrictions on the company's cash flow, operations or dividend payouts as a result of acquired debt?
(4)   What is the time commitment of the debt?
(5)   What is the company's working capital or liquidity position?
(6)   Is the debt/equity structure appropriate for this company?

It is important to note here that this list of questions is not all inclusive nor does it consider questions that require examination of the Balance Sheet in conjunction with the Statement of Income or other financial statements. These types of questions—for example, are the assets properly managed or what is the return on assets—will be examined in the chapter on the Statement of Income (Chapter 3) and the financial statement analysis section (Chapter 7.)

To answer the above questions, an investor must use various portions of the Balance Sheet. The Balance Sheet is comprised of three main categories: assets, liabilities and shareholder's equity. Each of these components have a specified order and arrangement as well as financial disclosure requirements. These requirements are dictated by generally accepted accounting principles or generally accepted industry standards.

In the following pages, information will be provided on each of the Balance Sheet components. This information will be followed by a discussion of the implications of the Balance Sheet elements from an investor's perspective.

Assets

Assets are the financial resources available to a firm to support and maintain business operations. They are normally obtained either through operations and earnings of the business, contributions to the business, or company borrowing.

Assets are normally arranged in their order of liquidity. Liquidity is defined as the length of time required to convert an asset to cash. Assets are listed with the most liquid first. That is why cash and cash equivalents are normally the first accounts listed on a Balance Sheet. Those accounts are followed by assets which can readily be converted to cash. For example, notes and accounts receivable are considered readily convertible to cash; either the customer or note holders are expected to pay within a short time period, or the receivable can be sold to a financial institution to obtain cash. Other current assets, such as inventory or prepaid insurance, are expected to be consumed within the operating cycle, often one year or less.

Any asset not listed as current is automatically long term. Long-term assets are usually categorized as either investments, property plant and equipment, intangibles, deferred charges or other (miscellaneous) assets. There is normally a specific order within each of these sub-account classifications as well, although the details of the specific accounts may or may not be listed in the published financial statements. For example, if the detailed information is shown within the property plant and equipment section, land will be listed before buildings and equipment. With potential industry exceptions noted, the order within the Balance Sheet accounts is fairly uniform.

The Investor's View of Assets

When an investor evaluates assets, they are primarily concerned with four key areas. The first question is "what is the nature of the asset?" For example, is it a long-term or short-term asset, how was the asset obtained and what is the asset used for? A second consideration is whether the level of asset investment is appropriate for this company? To illustrate, an investor may question why a manufacturing company has marketable securities comprising 25% of its total assets. Third, what is the value assigned to the asset and on what basis was this value determined? Generally accepted accounting principles allow a company to choose among alternative historical cost valuations for assigning inventory cost. When a company chooses among the acceptable alternatives, an investor needs to know the financial statement implications that result from that decision. The fourth question concerns the current market value of the assets.

Answers to each of these questions requires a more indepth look at a company's assets.

Current Assets

Cash and Cash Equivalents

The most liquid of resources, cash and cash equivalents are normally found as the first item on a Balance Sheet. They are classified as short-term assets since they are available for use immediately by the company. A company's cash balance is an item to be considered carefully. Under normal circumstances, a well-managed company will have minimal resources in cash and cash equivalents. Cash assets often represent underutilized resources and, in fact, can make a company an attractive take-over target. An advantage for an investor when considering the "cash" asset, is that the book value and market value of this asset are one and the same.

Marketable securities, often considered cash equivalents since they represent the short-term investment of excess idle funds, are valued at the lower of their historical cost or current market value. This is known in accounting jargon as LCM (Lower of Cost or Market.) The cost is the purchase price of the security on the date of acquisition, and the market value represents the current exchange price as of the date of the Balance Sheet. Thus it is easy to determine the value of such an asset.

Receivables

Receivables are the assets that arose as a result of an income generating process, i.e., the credit sales of the company. Since it is expected that the receivable will be collected within the normal operating cycle of the business, it is classified as a short-term asset.

A key consideration for the investor is the evaluation of the receivable balance in light of the sales generated by the company operating in a specific industry. A seasonal business with unique characteristics may produce Balance Sheet numbers that look unusual. However, barring unusual or seasonal industries, if the receivable balance on the year end Balance Sheet is large in relation to the sales for the year, it might indicate a credit or collection problem. Regardless of the type of problem, the outstanding receivables indicate a potential cash flow constraint. Such cash flow constraints are definitely of concern to an investor.

Another consideration for the investor is the valuation assigned to the receivables. The Balance Sheet dollars listed for receivables are the net of the gross receivables, adjusted for the allowance for uncollectible accounts. Its resulting book value, known as net realizable value, may or may not be an indication of the current market value should the receivables need to be sold in order to generate cash or to be pledged as collateral for a loan.

Inventory

The lifeline of manufacturing companies, inventory represents the company's investment in its goods for resale. Since it is expected that the asset will be sold within an operating cycle, it is usually classified as short term.

The normal evaluation of assets by investors becomes more important in the area of inventory. A critical issue is the proper level of inventory. Too much inventory results in increased carrying costs, and inventory shortages leave the company vulnerable to lost sales. The most important issue for an investor is whether the level of inventory is appropriate for a given company? To answer that question, the investor must consider such factors as seasonality, unique characteristics of a particular industry, competition, the state of the economy and the pace of inventory turnover.

An investor must also consider a company's cost structure and how it determines the inventory valuation. It is important to comprehend the specifics of the inventory valuation alternatives L.I.F.O. versus F.I.F.O. (last in, first out - first in, first out) and to understand how the company's inventory valuation method affects the financial statement elements. For example, companies with identical cost structures would indicate different Balance Sheet and Statement of Income numbers if one company chooses L.I.F.O. and the other chooses F.I.F.O.. The company who chooses F.I.F.O. will most likely report a higher inventory number and a lower cost of goods sold than the L.I.F.O. company assuming moderately increasing prices. Additional detailed information on inventory investment and cost structure can be found in the footnote disclosures accompanying the financial statements (see Appendix 1.)

Once the inventory cost determination is made, the Balance Sheet normally reflects a lower of that cost or a market valuation and, as such, provides the investor with an indication of the current market value if market is below cost.

Although a company may have other current asset accounts listed in addition to those discussed above, the balances in such accounts are normally not material to the company's financial position. As such, they are not usually a concern for investors.

Long-Term Assets

Investments

Investments listed on the Balance Sheet are normally funds invested in affiliated companies, advances to affiliated companies, purchases of stocks or bonds in other non-affiliated companies, long-term receivables and specific funds set aside for long-term projects, such as plant expansion or debt retirement.

Investments classified as long term are recorded in the accounting records at the cost at the date of acquisition. Subsequent to acquisition, investments such as the long-term project funds are increased for interest accumulated. Investments in affiliated companies are affected by whether or not the company exerts significant control over operations (in accordance with Accounting Principles Board (APB) Opinion #18.) If significant control is present, the equity method of accounting for the investment is required. If significant influence is not present, then the investment in equity securities is valued at the lower of cost or market. Once again, additional information is usually provided in the notes to the financial statements.

Property, Plant and Equipment

Property, plant and equipment represents the company's investment in its long-term operating facilities. Another name sometimes noted for this type of asset is "fixed assets." Assets sitting idle or awaiting resale are not classified as property, plant and equipment.

The Balance Sheet dollars shown for property, plant and equipment require scrutiny by investors. The "value" listed is in fact a book value, determined by the asset's original cost subsequently reduced by depreciation for each year that the asset was used. This depreciation process is nothing more than a periodic write-off of the asset cost over its estimated useful life. Obviously depreciation is not applicable to land holdings, but all plant and equipment requires annual depreciation write-offs. Thus, an asset held for 20 years may have little if any book value.

For an investor, depreciable assets represent an area where the asset value listed may not even be close to its replacement cost or current market value. In fact, in recent years many company takeovers have centered on such undervalued assets. Determining market values for such assets may be difficult for an investor but it is important to remember that the book value found on the Balance Sheet most likely represents an undervalued asset by current day standards.

Intangibles

Intangibles represent assets utilized in the company that do not have physical form or substance. That does not mean they are any less important. Rather, their value can in some cases be material since part of their value is the anticipated benefits in future periods. The most common intangible assets are patents, trademarks, franchises and goodwill.

The cost of acquiring an intangible depends upon the method of acquisition. For those intangibles purchased, it is simply the acquisition cost. For those intangibles developed within the company, such as a patent, the cost of the intangible is governed by Financial Accounting Standards Board (FASB) Statement #2. This statement requires the expensing of all in-house costs to develop the patent. Thus intangible costs for patents are limited to registration, accounting and legal fees generated by the registrations process or any legal costs incurred to defend such a patent.

Perhaps the item of greatest interest to the investor is goodwill. This intangible arises when the acquisition cost of a company is in excess of the book value of the net assets purchased. Goodwill has become more significant in recent years caused by the wave of mergers and acquisitions.

Intangibles require a periodic write-off, called amortization, in a manner similar to that of depreciation of plant and equipment. The write-off period is the economic useful life of the intangible, usually not to exceed 40 years. As a result, the number reflected on the Balance Sheet is the unamortized residual balance of the intangible. To an investor, this book value may appear to be rather meaningless, and due to the nature of intangibles, it is very difficult for an investor to determine a current market value. That does not mean an investor should simply ignore intangibles. Rather the investor should look at the existence of intangibles as an indication of potential future benefits and try to ascertain the value of such benefits to the company.

Liabilities

Liabilities are the financial obligations of a business incurred to support and maintain the business operations. They normally arise as a result of a financing transaction in conjunction with the acquisition of a company asset. Liabilities are normally arranged in their order of maturity, i.e., when the obligation becomes due. Those debts which mature within one year or the operating cycle whichever is longer (again as a practical matter, within one year) are classified as current or short-term liabilities. Those maturing in excess of a year are listed as long-term liabilities. In the liability section, there is not usually any further sub-classification for long-term liabilities as there was in the long-term asset section of the Balance Sheet.

The Investor's View of Liabilities

When an investor evaluates liabilities, they are primarily concerned with four key areas. The first concern is the nature of the liability, i.e., what was the source of the liability and what is the time frame for repayment. A second issue is to consider the debt and equity structure, i.e., what percentage of the asset base is supported by debt versus that supported by equity? This determination is aided by calculation of the debt/equity ratio, which will be discussed in Chapter 7. The third area is the evaluation of the level of debt and whether it is appropriate for a particular company in a specific industry. The final issue focuses on the financial and operating restrictions imposed as a result of any debt obligations. Any such restrictions are of particular concern to an investor since the restriction may affect the company's financing capabilities as well as the ability to pay dividends.

Answers to each of these questions requires a more in-depth look at a company's liability section of the Balance Sheet in conjunction with the notes to the financial statements.

Current Liabilities

Current liabilities are the obligations due within the next year. They often arise as a result of current operating costs, for example, accrued payroll, accounts payable or taxes due. Additional types of current liabilities are short-term loans and the current portion of long-term debt due within the next year. This debt is reclassified from the long-term debt section of the Balance Sheet each year.

An investor's view of liabilities is normally balanced with an examination of the current assets. It is those assets classified as current which represent the ideal source of funds to repay the current liabilities. Any company who cannot support their current debt obligation with the current resources available may not represent an appropriate investment.

Current assets less current liabilities is commonly known as net working capital. Working capital is of prime interest to investors as well as to creditors. In many instances, credit agreements and loan covenants require a certain level of working capital. A company's failure to meet such a requirement can directly affect a stockholder's interest by restricting a company's financing options. This limitation thereby restricts growth opportunities which may be beneficial to an investor's interest. In addition, such agreements often carry dividend payout restrictions, thereby limiting investor's returns. Information on such loan covenants can usually be found in the notes to the financial statements.

Long-Term Liabilities

Long-term liabilities are the financial obligations whose repayment terms are in excess of one year. These obligations normally result from a company's financing decisions concerning operations and future growth.

These liabilities are often in the form of notes, mortgages, bonds, and long-term capital lease obligations.

Additional long-term debt that is often seen but not part of a company's financing decision is deferred taxes. Deferred taxes presently represent a temporary postponement of the federal tax obligation to a period exceeding one year from the Balance Sheet date. (Currently, the Financial Accounting Standards Board has delayed implementation of Statement #96 concerning deferred taxes until 1992. This statement will have significant impact on the Balance Sheet and Statement of Income presentations.)

Significant changes in pension accounting, dictated by the Financial Accounting Standards Board Statement #87, also affected the financial statement presentation for pensions. Under this statement, a long-term liability may also exist for the underfunding of a company's pension plan. If the amount funded (i.e., sent to a pension trust) in a given year is less than the pension expense recorded, a liability (usually long term) must be shown on the Balance Sheet. (In an instance where the opposite is true, i.e., the amount funded exceeds the current expense, the difference is reflected as a long-term asset.)

A word of caution is necessary here. The above statement is a very simplified summary of pensions and how it affects the Balance Sheet. Corresponding changes in the note disclosure requirements concerning pensions have also occurred and will be discussed in Chapter 6. Please keep in mind that the present accounting and reporting regulations concerning pensions are extremely complex and well beyond the scope of this book. For additional information, please consult a current volume of an intermediate accounting text, or other authoritative accounting literature.

An investor should examine the debt section of the Balance Sheet very carefully. Of prime importance is the level of debt the company maintains. A company which finances its asset base with 80% debt may not represent a viable investment due to the large commitment of resources necessary to satisfy the debt. A high level of debt, with its corresponding covenant restrictions, often limits the future options of a company. The inability to satisfy the debt can only yield bankruptcy. It is also possible that the company has too little debt. At first this may seem strange, but there are times when a company's unwillingness to carry debt restricts their growth opportunities. An investor must look at a company's debt structure and try to determine whether the level of debt is appropriate.

Shareholder's Equity

Often called stockholder's equity, shareholder's equity represents the residual interest after liabilities are subtracted from assets. The amount listed for shareholder's equity in no way indicates the value of the firm. It is simply a measurement of the net ownership interest that arose as a result of capital contributions, earnings retained in the business, and any distributions to owners.

Typically, shareholder's equity is considered to be listed in the order of decreasing permanency. This simply means that from a legal perspective, preferred and common stock par value is recorded at issuance and is considered legal capital. These accounts are the last to be affected by a bankruptcy or liquidation.

Preferred and common stock accounts are usually followed by any additional contributed capital received from the sale of stock. This amount represents the dollars received at issuance in excess of the par or stated value of the preferred or common stock. The amount is the difference between the market price and the par or stated value of the stock certificate. If no-par stock has been issued, there is no additional contributed capital as a result of the transaction.

The last account listed in shareholder's equity is retained earnings which represents the net of profits, losses, and dividends declared over the life of the organization. Once again, the value noted for such accounts represents an accumulated interest, and not a book or market value.

There can be other shareholder's equity accounts listed, for example, treasury stock. This account reflects the temporary reacquisition cost to the organization to repurchase its own shares in the market. It is actually a contra-shareholder's equity account. This means that the value assigned to the treasury stock is a reduction of the total shareholder's equity. Companies reacquire their own stock for a variety of reasons. For example, if the present stock price is too low, a good way to boost the company's stock price is to use excess cash to repurchase their own stock. Another common reason for repurchasing one's own stock is to delay or eliminate a potential takeover of the company.

There has been some concern of late that the Balance Sheet information is too limited concerning the shareholder equity accounts. Many companies have countered this by preparing an actual Statement of Changes in Shareholder Equity, or by providing the equivalent information of such a statement in the notes to the financial statements. As a result, information on the changes in each of these accounts is often available. See Chapter 5 for a discussion on the Statement of Changes in Shareholder Equity.

Other Balance Sheet Considerations

The above discussion highlights the classification and valuation of each section of the Balance Sheet. One must consider that the Balance Sheet represents the account balances at a point in time after all financial transactions have been recorded. Thus it is the impact of the transaction, not the detailed transaction itself, that is reflected on a Balance Sheet.

Given the detailed nature of the Balance Sheet, it is tempting to try and identify one major or most important section of the Balance Sheet. This however, is not possible. Depending upon one's perspective, i.e., a banker, trade creditor or investor, various areas of the Balance Sheet have various levels of significance. For example, a trade creditor wishing to sell supplies to a company on credit, would most likely examine the asset base (specifically accounts receivable, inventory and property plant and equipment) to determine if the company is managing their assets effectively. They would also determine whether any assets are available as collateral to satisfy a defaulted debt obligation if one should occur.

Investors will often examine a company's Balance Sheet to determine the value or worth of a company. The result of such a determination will be used as a basis for a stock purchase. Although there are many areas that an investor would examine, (certainly not limited to the Balance Sheet), the primary Balance Sheet focus would be on working capital and working capital requirements. An investor would also be interested in the capital structure of a company, as shown by the debt and equity components.

Many financial statement readers do not look at the Balance Sheet alone, rather they examine the Balance Sheet in conjunction with the remainder of the financial statement package. As a result, the subsequent chapters examine each of the remaining components of the financial statement package.

Limitations of Balance Sheet Data

The Balance Sheet provides investors with information on the financial resources and obligations of a company. However, it is critical to remember that there are limitations to such information.

The Balance Sheet represents a static statement, i.e., account balances at a specific point in time. The information is not relevant to any other time period. This limitation can be overcome to some degree by obtaining more than a single Balance Sheet for a company. Examination of financial information for a single time period is relatively meaningless; it is the comparison of several financial statements that can provide investors with an overall view of the financial structure of a firm.

An additional consideration is the data source for the Balance Sheet information. All reported financial information is an output of the accounting system and is a recording of transactions that have already been completed. The type of information investors need often goes beyond the recording of past events. However, armed with the knowledge of past events, investors can usually utilize that information in their assessment of the company as a potential or on-going investment.

Another issue for the investor to consider is the value assigned to the assets which are reflected on the Balance Sheet. These numbers are not usually indicative of the current market or replacement value of such assets. As a result, examination of the Balance Sheet does not answer questions on the present value of a company's assets.

Other Financial Statements

Many investors do not look at the Balance Sheet alone, rather they examine the Balance Sheet in conjunction with the remainder of the financial statement package. As a result, the subsequent chapters examine each of the remaining elements of the financial statement package, beginning with the Statement of Income in Chapter 3.

THE STATEMENT OF INCOME

The Statement of Income is a report of a company's revenues, expenses, and gains and losses that are the result of operating and non-operating activities over a period of time. Another name commonly noted for such a statement is The Statement of Earnings. Older terminology, often referred to internally by the veterans of the finance and accounting environment, is the Profit and Loss Statement (P & L). This title however, is not usually found in published financial statements. It is also possible that an investor will see a statement called Statement of Income and Retained Earnings. This statement simply combines two of the generally accepted financial statements into one.

Income Statement Basics

A Statement of Income (see Appendix 1) provides an investor with information on the company's current-period operating activity. In addition, it will usually indicate whether that activity is from normal operations or incidental transactions. Normal operations are the repetitive revenues and expenses of a firm, earned or incurred in their main line of business. For example, a company that is producing sweaters will have sales (revenues) from their product and incur costs (expenses) associated with producing and selling those sweaters.

Incidental transactions are the revenues, expenses, gains or losses earned or incurred by a company outside of their normal operating activity. To illustrate, a company invests its excess idle cash in marketable securities. As a result of that investment decision, they earn investment income. Since their primary operations are the manufacturing of sweaters, investment income—although it is a current period activity—is incidental to their main business purpose.

Those activities which are considered normal operations are of greater interest to the investor, since they provide an indication of the company's core strength. An investor is concerned that the main products of the business are being produced and sold successfully which is necessary to ensure the on-going existence of the firm. That is not to say that the investor does not care about the other types of transactions, but the main focus is on the on-going core operations necessary to sustain the firm over the long term.

The financial transactions that are summarized on the Statement of Income directly impact the many account balances reported on the Balance Sheet. For example, the net of the revenues, expenses, and gains and losses is shown as "net income" on the bottom of the Statement of Income. This net income figure also carries forward and is shown on the Statement of Changes in Shareholder's Equity as one element which causes an increase in the balance of retained earnings for the period (assuming a profit, a decrease if the result is a loss). See Appendix 2 for an illustration of the relationship between net income as reported on the Statement of Income and the impact on Retained Earnings as reported in the Statement of Changes in Shareholder's Equity.

It is also important to note that The Statement of Income will show both repetitive and non-repetitive type transactions. Repetitive transactions are those that can usually be expected to occur in each operating period, and can be either normal operations or incidental transactions. For example, sales, payroll expense, and interest income usually occur every operating period. Non-repetitive transactions are those that are unusual and infrequent in nature and are often incidental transactions. To illustrate, a company sells idle plant and equipment and recognizes a gain on the transaction. This gain is not expected to occur again in the near future since the plant and equipment it relates to has been sold. An investor must recognize that non-repetitive gains and losses can distort the long-term profit picture of the company.

How and When Is a Statement of Income Prepared?

A Statement of Income reports the results of a period of time, usually a month, a quarter or a year. As a result, this statement is normally dated "for the period ended" on the last day of the accounting report period. If a company is issuing quarterly financials at the end of the first quarter, the Statement of Income will be dated "for the quarter ended March 31, 19XX"; if it is an annual report, the statement will be dated "for the year ended December 31, 19XX."

The balances reflected as account totals on the Statement of Income reflect the sum of the transactions in those accounts during the reporting period. Thus, these account totals represent an accumulated balance which is the result of on-going activities, measured and reported upon based on a designated reporting period and in accordance with standard accounting conventions. This is in contrast to the account totals reported on the Balance Sheet, which were reported as of one specific date and were relevant only on that particular day.

The actual preparation of the Statement of Income usually takes place several days past the last day of the accounting reporting period, in order to ensure that all of the accounting transactions have been accumulated. Once again, practical constraints make this process a necessity.

In a manner similar to the Balance Sheet preparation, the Statement of Income is usually prepared monthly for the company's operating managers. Publication of the Statement of Income to those outside of the company usually takes place at quarter-end and/or year-end when overall disclosure of the company's finances occurs. In contrast to the published Balance Sheet, there is no "standard" requirement governing presentation and format of the Statement of Income, other than the inclusion of key income statement elements (revenues, expenses, gains and losses) which must be present. These elements have been identified and defined by the Statement of Financial Accounting Concepts #6.

It is important to remember that the overall objective of all financial statements, particularly the Statement of Income, is to report on the financial activities of the company. Because the activities reported on the Statement of Income do not necessarily lend themselves to "standardization," the need for flexibility is present. However, the need for flexibility must be balanced by the need for full disclosure of the financial events.

The Statement of Income usually takes one of two forms: either the single step or the multiple-step presentation. Both of these presentation formats are widely used and universally accepted. In addition, some companies have chosen to report their Statement of Income using a combination of the two. Since there is no generally accepted accounting principle dictating the form and presentation, almost any report format which contains the key income statement items identified above, is considered acceptable. This assumes of course, that the objective of full disclosure reporting, i.e., identifying all the information necessary for an investor to make an informed investment decision, is present.

A single-step format on the Statement of Income (as shown in Appendix 1) groups all revenues and gains together and classifies them as total revenues. It correspondingly groups expenses and losses together as total costs, and the net of the two is identified as net income (this statement assumes that there are no extraordinary items to be reported). Obviously the primary advantage of this method is its simplicity. However, a disadvantage lies in the "gross" grouping of transactions that may have no relevance to each other. From an investors perspective, this process could mask some critical financial data.

A multiple step-format on the Statement of Income groups the key financial statement elements according to the nature of the transaction. As a result, the statement is further broken down into sub-sections. The first section in a multiple-step statement reports the results of the primary sales operations, i.e., sales and the cost of the sales, with the net of these elements identified as gross profit. Operating expenses, such as selling or administrative expenses, are the next grouping reported followed by a sub-total called "income from continuing operations," or "income from primary operations." This number is important to an investor, since it identifies a measure of a company's operating viability, regardless of the incidental transactions described earlier.

Further delineation of the Statement of Income continues, with the reporting of the incidental revenues, expenses, gains and losses which are often identified as "other" revenues, gains etc.

Income before taxes is clearly identified and any discontinued operations, extraordinary items, or changes in accounting principle are reported separately (net of tax) before net income is shown. The primary advantage of such detail in a multiple-step statement is the amount of information available for use by the investor.

Regardless of a single-step or a multiple-step presentation, every Statement of Income will identify unusual or infrequent items as well as extraordinary gains and losses and changes in accounting principles. In addition, all statements are required to show earnings per share information on the face of the Statement of Income in accordance with the Accounting Principles Board Opinion #15. See Appendix 2 for sample single-step and multiple-step Statement of Income presentations.

Each of the elements reported on the Statement of Income, as well as the mechanism used to report them, have repercussions for the investor. The remainder of this chapter will examine the investor's perspective and needs for financial information from the Statement of Income.

How Does an Investor Use the Statement of Income?

Investors are primarily concerned with two aspects of an investment: the dividend earnings that will be received from such an investment and the capital appreciation of the stock. Both of these concerns require an investor to obtain and analyze the Statement of Income information. An investor will usually have questions about a company's operations:

specifically, the level of earnings, the nature or source of such earnings, and the trend of the earnings as well as the potential of future earnings. An investor assessment is often facilitated by performing financial statement analysis, often ratio analysis, on the Statement of Income. Ratio and financial statement analysis will be explored in detail in Chapter 7.

Key information found on the Statement of Income, combined with the notes to the financial statements (see Chapter 6 for additional information on note disclosures), provides answers to questions often asked by investors. Other sources of information, such as earnings forecasts, industry statistics and economic indicators, will also have to be utilized to assess investment quality and value. Important questions asked by investors are as follows:

(1) What are the reported earnings for the period?
(2) Are the reported earnings adequate in terms of the asset base maintained by the company?
(3) Will the reported earnings generate enough cash to warrant a dividend payout?
(4) What is the source of the earnings, i.e., are they from primary and continuing operations or are the result of non-recurring transactions?
(5) What has been the earnings trend in the last 5-10 years?
(6) What are the projected future earnings?
(7) What are the general economic and industry conditions and how do they affect the earnings forecasts?
(8) Is the firm diversified in its operations?
(9) What is the relationship between revenue and cost trends?
(10) What is the return on the company's assets?
(11) To what extent is leverage being used and what is the degree of risk associated with this leverage?

All of these questions deal with earnings and the earning potential of a company, but all of the information is not readily available on the Statement of Income. An investor will, however, need to understand and utilized the information reported on the Statement of Income as a starting point for the earnings analysis. Although The Statement of Income is a historical statement—i.e., a record of past earnings, and its information may be somewhat limiting for an investor's future projections—without the Statement of Income as a basis, further analysis is of doubtful value.

In the following pages, information will be provided on the various components of the Statement of Income. This information will be followed by a discussion of the relevance of each component to an investor's analysis.

Sales, Cost of Goods Sold and Gross Profit

Sales, and the resulting profits, are the primary reason a company is in business. The dollar value of sales reported on the Statement of Income represents the accumulated balance of primary revenue earned by the company during a specified time period. It is essential to note the word "earned," which normally means that revenue is reported when legal title to the merchandise has passed to the customer (usually designated by the FOB point specified in the shipping terms) or when services have been rendered to the consumer. This recognition of sales is governed by what is known in accounting terms as the revenue principle.

An important distinction for investors to comprehend is that sales are not usually recorded at the point of cash collection unless cash is exchanged at the time of the sale. If the sale takes place (i.e., the rendering of services or the shipment of merchandise) with a promise of cash in the future, the resulting balance owed by the customer, known as Accounts Receivable, can be found on the Balance Sheet. If collection of cash occurs prior to the shipment of goods or the rendering of services, no revenue is recorded and a liability for the cash received is reflected on the Balance Sheet. Thus revenue recognition is not governed by cash collections rather it is governed by the performance of the services or the shipment of merchandise.

Cost of goods sold reflects all the costs incurred by the company in order to generate sales. Recognition of such costs is governed by the matching principle which requires the offset of expenses against the revenue reported. Some of the expenses recorded in cost of goods sold are obvious, others are not. For example, the cost of the materials used in the manufacturing process are obviously a production cost, and are therefore transferred to cost of goods sold when the product is sold. However, the depreciation cost for the machinery used in production is also considered a "product" cost and is usually assigned as a cost in the allocation of overhead. It is important to remember that there are many components of production cost which are reflected in the accounting for costs of goods sold.

Gross profit, often noted as gross margin, is the difference between sales and cost of sales. This number represents the residual value available to offset the remaining operating costs of the company. Many financial statement readers spend a great deal of time on the analysis of gross profit, its value, its trend and its implications for a company.

The Investor's View of Sales, Cost of Goods Sold and Gross Profit

An investor is primarily concerned with the earnings of a company and earnings are directly affected by the reported sales, cost of goods sold and gross profit. However, an investor cannot be successful in the evaluation of earnings without several sequential income statements. Analysis of any Statement of Income element requires a comparison of the reporting element from accounting period to accounting period in order to determine the trend in the reported activities. Thus, an investor considers change over time, rather than any one reported figure, to be critical in an earnings analysis.

Sales

The overall objective of analyzing the Statement of Income and its reported profit begins with the current sales data. An investor obviously must look at sales in conjunction with the cost structure. However, sales trends alone can also be an important indicator of a company's performance. The expected pattern is one of growth in sales, since growth in sales with either a corresponding level of growth in costs or even a decreased relative cost caused by economies of scale, should yield higher profits to the firm.

A further consideration is the life-cycle of the company and of the industry. Sales levels and sales trends within a mature company or industry must be evaluated differently than sales from an emerging company or industry. Stagnant sales levels, or sales growth below that of their competitors in the industry, or even sales patterns contrary to current economic conditions, should indicate the need for closer examination by the investor. To obtain the best information possible, sales trends should be examined for at least 5 years, and 10 years if possible. The information on sales and sales trends is relatively easy to find in the annual report. Such information can be found in the section titled either Financial Review or Financial Summary.

However, it is important to examine the reported sales growth closely to determine the exact cause of the reported increase. Increases in reported sales can be caused by two different factors: an increase in actual units sold or an increase caused by a change in the selling price, or possibly a combination of the two. A further consideration is determining changes in sales by the various product lines. An overall increase in reported sales can mask an actual decline in one particular product line which may have implications for an investor. Obviously, an investor needs to know the cause of any reported change in sales.

It is also important to remember that an investor cannot look at sales trends alone, but must closely examine the changes in the cost of goods sold as well.

Cost of Goods Sold

Cost of goods sold (also identified as cost of sales) is often considered critical information on the Statement of Income. Sales increases alone do not contribute dollar for dollar to the net income of a firm unless the cost structure is closely maintained and costs closely monitored.

Cost of goods sold is determined by adding the beginning inventory value to the net current purchases (or production costs of a manufacturer) and subtracting the inventory still on hand. Thus whatever was available at the beginning of the period, added to the current period activity, is either still on hand (reported as ending inventory on the Balance Sheet) or it must be reflected as a cost of sales during the current period.

The principle item affecting a company's reported cost of sales is the inventory cost method chosen by a company. The two primary methods used are L.I.F.O.(last-in, first-out) and F.I.F.O. (first-in, first-out). Each of these two methods has certain advantages and disadvantages, depending upon the general price trends of the goods purchased or produced for inventory.

For example, in a period of rising prices, L.I.F.O. actually results in lower taxes, because it assigns the most recent (higher) costs to the cost of goods sold on the Statement of Income, thereby reducing income before taxes and income tax expense. The inverse of that, however, is that the reported value for inventory on the Balance Sheet is at lower, often unrealistic prices. This may cause a potential understatement of the asset value, which is important for an investor to recognize.

F.I.F.O. on the other hand, has the opposite impact. During rising prices, the older (lower) dollar values are assigned to cost of goods sold. This results in higher reported profits. The corresponding impact on the Balance Sheet is a current valuation for inventory.

How does a company pick an inventory cost methodology? It is traditionally thought that in any period of rising prices, the benefit of reduced taxes will cause a firm to choose the L.I.F.O. method. However, it is important for an investor to realize that if a company chooses to use L.I.F.O. for tax purposes, the IRS requires that they also use L.I.F.O. for financial reporting purposes. Thus, the benefit of reduced taxes causes lower reported profits to the shareholder's as well. However, some companies are choosing L.I.F.O. and reporting supplemental disclosures indicating what the income would have been had they chosen the F.I.F.O.

method. This allows the benefits of both methods, i.e., lower actual income taxes and disclosure of higher reported profits to the shareholders.

Although many may argue the advantages and disadvantages of L.I.F.O. versus F.I.F.O., it is important for an investor to understand both The Statement of Income and Balance Sheet impact of the company's chosen inventory cost method. In the event that a company chooses to change methods, an investor should note that a one-time gain or loss will result and will be reflected in the portion of the Statement of Income reporting changes in accounting principle. This one time transaction can distort the earnings trends of the company and earnings must be evaluated in this light. More discussion on changes in accounting principle can be found later in this chapter.

Gross Profit

Gross profit is the net of sales and cost of goods sold and is often considered a barometer of a company's operational efficiency since it represents profit after direct production costs. Gross profit dollars are basically meaningless; it is the gross profit percentage or the gross margin percentage that is the subject of much analysis.

For example, assume a company has sales and cost of sales as follows:

	1989	1990
Sales	$600,000	$750,000
Cost of Sales	400,000	520,000
Gross Profit	$200,000	$230,000

Given this information, the reported gross profit dollars increased from $200,000 to $230,000. However, it is important to examine the information in relative terms. Performing such an analysis shows that although the sales increased 25%, the cost of sales actually increased 30%, thus the gross profit percentage actually declined from 33.3% to 30.6%. This illustration shows why it is always important to look at the relative changes in related financial statement accounts.

Why does gross profit and its corresponding change interest investors? Changes in gross profit indicate either a change in sales price, sales volume or the company's cost structure. To obtain a thorough understanding of the company's operations, an investor must be able to identify and understand the cause and effect of such changes.

Increases in gross profit dollars increase funds available for current operating expenses. As a result of changes in sales patterns, an investor might expect to see corresponding changes in current operating expenses.

Operating Expenses

Operating expenses can be described as expenses incurred in the business other than cost of goods sold and unusual or infrequent items. Typically they include such costs as selling, general and administrative, depreciation expense (other than the component included as part of cost of goods sold), and research and development costs. Within selling, general and administrative are costs associated with employees (other than production employees), i.e., salaries and their benefits. Also included are office expenses, travel, advertising, rent and bad debt expense.

Depreciation Expense

Depreciation expense can be a significant component of the Statement of Income. In Chapter 1, the impact of different depreciation methods chosen by a company were examined (see pages 5 and 6). Depreciation expense is the charge against current period revenue for the use of plant and equipment during that time period. For example, if a company purchases equipment that they will use for 10 years, they do not charge equipment expense in the year of purchase since they will receive benefits from that equipment for a 10 year period. Rather, the cost of the equipment is spread over its useful life through the depreciation charges recorded. Additional information on depreciation expense is reported in the footnotes to the financial statements. Investor's should note that depreciation reported on the Statement of Income usually does not match the depreciation recorded for federal income tax purposes.

Financial accounting concepts and IRS regulations require a charge against current revenue for the cost of plant and equipment because the value of such an asset benefits many accounting periods. There are various ways to calculate depreciation for accounting as well as tax purposes. Straight-line depreciation (i.e., an even periodic write-off) is available for tax purposes but most companies use an accelerated method, such as ACRS (Accelerated Cost Recovery System) or the current tax law depreciation MACRS (Modified Accelerated Cost Recovery System). These methods are governed by tax law and are calculated in the IRS regulations. Accordingly, investors will not see the results of tax depreciation methods since they are utilized only in the tax return.

For financial reporting purposes, most companies utilize straight-line depreciation. This method calculates an even amount of depreciation over the life of the asset. For example, a $500,000 piece of equipment with an estimated 5 year life and no salvage value will cause a depreciation charge of $100,000 a year for each of the 5 years of asset life (this assumes the machine is used for 5 years).

Accelerated methods do exist for financial reporting purposes, but are not often used by companies. Accelerated depreciation permits higher expense charges in the earlier years of the asset. The higher expenses correspondingly reduce reported earnings. Since depreciation for financial reporting purposes and tax purposes do not have to be the same, many companies choose straight-line for financial reporting purposes and accelerated methods for tax purposes. This maximizes both their financial reporting and tax positions.

Research and Development Expense

The dollars shown on the Statement of Income for Research and Development (R & D) represent the company's cost of maintaining an on-going research and development function. Dollars charged to such an account represent all costs incurred in maintaining R & D activities, including personnel, equipment costs (unless the equipment has another function within the company), and materials. Depending upon the industry, the R & D expense of a company can be a substantial charge against earnings. An investor must examine a company's R & D commitment in light of short-term and long-term goals of the company. This topic is discussed in detail in the next section on the investor's view of operating expenses.

There may be other types of operating expenses listed on a Statement of Income, such as discontinued operations, interest expense and others. However, many companies classify interest expense as "other income and expenses" rather than operating expenses. This will be discussed in the section entitled "Other Income and Expenses."

The Investor's View of Operating Expenses

An investor should carefully examine the section on operating expenses. Each operating expense has a different connotation for an investor to consider.

Selling, general and administrative expenses are a large component of operating expenses, and should be related to the sales activity during the period. If sales increase, one might expect selling expenses to increase as well, but it is the proportionate increase an investor must consider. For example, a change in corporate credit policy may provide increased credit for customers which in turn may have been a factor in increasing sales. However, if the bad-debt expense for the period has increased beyond the relative sales increase, an investor should question the value of such a policy. One would also expect an increase in commissions to be related to an increase in sales, thereby reflecting a higher personnel cost in the Selling, General and Administrative element of the Statement of Income.

If an investor identifies increased costs associated with Selling, General and Administrative costs, without a corresponding increase in sales, closer examination may be necessary. This situation does not necessarily mean that the company is having difficulty containing its costs. It may be that the company is trying to enter a new market, service its existing clients better, or prepare for an introduction of a new product. An investor should determine that over time, a relationship between sales and the costs associated with that sales level exists and is maintained.

An investor's view of depreciation expense is somewhat limited and is actually a function of the company's investment in plant and equipment. Thus, the Balance Sheet valuation for plant and equipment must be examined in conjunction with the current period operating charges for depreciation.

A company's commitment to their plant and equipment is manifested in their philosophy of maintaining and replacing such assets. An investor needs to examine whether the assets are being replaced at the proper intervals in order to maintain the company's competitive position. If a company has minimal expense associated with depreciation, chances are that their asset base is of advanced age and may need replacement. If additional resources are not made available for asset purchase, the company's competitive position may be hampered. This has obvious implications in an investors evaluation of a company's operation.

An investor should also examine the role of Research and Development (R & D) of a company within the context of the specific industry. Certain industries, such as high-tech industries, spend a great deal on R & D in any given year, whereas companies in a "mature" industry may not be committed to such expenditures. An investor must evaluate R & D and its relationship to a product line, to the existing market conditions, and even relative to the firm's competition. To remain an on-going, viable operation, many companies must commit resources for R & D. Similar to the philosophy of asset replacement, a company's competitive position may be hampered without such a commitment.

A company's commitment to research and development is of particular concern to an investor since R & D expense lowers profits when incurred. If the R & D dollars are well spent, the long term reward in terms of profits may be substantial if it allows the company to maintain or improve its competitive position. In contrast, a company may not be able to maintain a high level of R & D expenditures. Although there is a positive impact on short-term earnings since expenses will be lower, profits in the long-term may suffer.

After operating expenses have been subtracted from primary revenues, the result is identified as "income from operations" or simply "operating income." This number identifies the profit before taxes from the company's main line of business, i.e., their primary operations. Assuming an investor desires an investment that will yield both current dividends and long-term capital growth, the company must indicate its ability to generate profits from its primary operations. Although other income and expense items will also appear on the Statement of Income, they are often identified in a separate section of the statement.

Other Income and Expenses

This section of the Statement of Income is reserved for unusual or infrequent items or transactions of an incidental nature. For example, it is in this section that interest income or interest expense will often appear (although some companies prefer to classify interest expense as an operating expense). Other commonly noted items are the gains and losses recognized on incidental transactions, such as the sale of an asset.

An investor may have limited interest in such information, except for interest expense. Interest expense may be evaluated in terms of the cost of borrowing for the firm, and it may be an indication of the level of debt and the company's ability to carry such debt. If the interest expense is large in proportion to the other reported expense or income figures, it may indicate a company is overburdened by debt. Determination of the appropriate level of debt must consider many factors, not just the reported interest expense.

Discontinued Operations, Extraordinary Items and Changes in Accounting Principle

Investors will often see information in the lower portion of the Statement of Income identified as discontinued operations, an extraordinary gain or loss, or the cumulative effect of changes in accounting principle. These items are specifically identified as required by generally accepted accounting principles.

Discontinued operations will reflect the profit or loss associated with the disposal of a business segment while extraordinary items are transactions that are both an unusual nature and infrequent in occurrence. For example, a loss due to natural disaster, providing it is unusual for that location and infrequent in occurrence would be classified as extraordinary.

Changes in accounting principle occur when a company changes from one generally accepted accounting principle to another. For example, a change in depreciation methods, from an accelerated method to straight-line, will cause a change in accounting principle. A change from one inventory method to another, such as L.I.F.O. to F.I.F.O. previously discussed, is also classified as a change in accounting principle. As a result, the cumulative effect of such changes must be calculated an identified as a separate item on the Statement of Income.

What do discontinued operations, extraordinary items and changes in accounting principle mean to an investor? Overall, they represent unusual items that are not expected to reoccur and, as such, should be isolated by the investor when evaluating a company's financial statements. However, discontinued operations should be of particular interest to an investor since the associated costs usually depress reported earnings and it signifies a reduced commitment to a business segment. An investor must consider whether this decision represents a permanent reduction in total operating capacity or a spin-off of a segment that is incompatible with the operating objectives of the company. Either way, this item warrants consideration by an investor.

Earnings per Share (EPS)

Earnings per share appears on the Statement of Income, usually as a separate section after Net Income. EPS is shown for Income from Operations and Net Income. If there are reportable items, such as extraordinary items or changes in accounting principle, EPS is normally shown for that item as well.

Two EPS amounts are usually shown on the face of the Statement of Income; primary EPS and fully diluted EPS. Primary EPS takes into account all securities which are determined to be common stock equivalents (CSE) and whose conversion would result in an increased number of shares of common stock outstanding. This determination is the result of a complex series of evaluations and calculations involving the convertible debt and equity securities.

Fully diluted EPS takes into account all potentially dilutive securities whether or not they are determined to be common stock equivalents. Thus fully diluted EPS will always be less than primary EPS.

The evaluation of potentially dilutive securities is a complex topic that goes well beyond the scope of this book. However, an investor can evaluate EPS as the earnings of the firm relative to a share of stock. Some investors may confuse EPS with dividends per share of stock, which is the result of the Board of Directors dividend declaration policy, or the market value or the stock. However, EPS is simply a summary figure indicating how much a company earned per share of stock.

Other Statement of Income Considerations

The Statement of Income has been described in detail in the preceding pages. However, for the information to be particularly useful for investors, several reporting periods must be obtained and compared. Enhancement of the comparison between periods can be accomplished by recasting the information into "common-size" statements. That simply converts each Statement of Income item into relative terms, usually equated as a percentage of sales. Using common-size information allows an investor to readily see any changes in an account as well as the potential impact of the change on related accounts. Showing such data as a percentage of sales also allows the investor to more clearly see the relationship between costs and revenues.

Limitations of Statement of Income Data

Contrary to Balance Sheet preparation, the Statement of Income does not have standard reporting requirements, other than that revenues, expenses, gains and losses must be reported. As a result of this lack of standardization, comparability between financial statements may be hampered. For example, one company may choose to report its interest expense as part of their operating costs, while another classifies interest as an other expense item.

A further limitation of Statement of Income data is actually caused by choices made in the actual recording of the transaction prior to its presentation in the financial statement. In Chapter 1, the issue of alternative depreciation methodologies in accounting and financial reporting was addressed while in this chapter, tax and financial reporting methods of depreciation were compared. In addition, the differences caused by inventory costing alternatives and its impact on the cost of goods sold reported on the Statement of Income were discussed earlier in this chapter. Each of these choices causes difficulty for an investor trying to compare financial information. Because companies record depreciation and cost of goods sold under different methods, allowed under generally accepted accounting principles, comparability of financial data is hampered. The Statement of Income will show an expense, but the information on the method used to calculate such an expense is often limited and appears only in the footnote disclosures. If an investor wishes to compare information of this type, it may not be possible to make a meaningful comparison.

A further limitation, and perhaps the most important limitation for an investor, is recognition of the Statement of Income as a record of past events. An investor needs to determine the earnings and growth potential of a company in order to judge its investment caliber. However, to effectively accomplish this, information on past earnings of the company is only one part of the puzzle. The use of additional information that goes beyond the standard financial statements will be necessary.

Other Financial Statement Data

The Balance Sheet and the Statement of Income form a data base. However, additional information can be obtained from examining the remaining parts of the financial statement package, beginning with the Statement of Cash Flows in Chapter 4.

THE STATEMENT OF CASH FLOWS

The Statement of Cash Flows reports the results of a company's business operations on a cash basis and is the only financial statement that reports information in this way. The cash basis statement is in contrast to the accounting records and the other financial statements which report on an accrual basis. As a result, the Statement of Cash Flows is unique.

Although the Statement of Cash Flows is cash based and the remainder of the financial statements are accrual based, there is a connecting link between the Statement of Cash Flows and the Balance Sheet. The beginning and ending cash balances shown on the Statement of Cash Flows must agree with the amount of cash listed as a current asset on the Balance Sheet. An important link also exists between the Statement of Cash Flows and the Statement of Income. When the Statement of Cash Flows is prepared using the indirect method (details of that method will be explained in the following pages), the net income figure reported on the Statement of Income is the starting figure for determining cash flows from operating activity on the Statement of Cash Flows. (See Appendix 2 for a diagram of the relationship of the Statement of Cash Flows to the Balance Sheet and Statement of Income.)

Cash Flow Basics

Before a discussion of the Statement of Cash Flows begins, it is helpful to summarize the basics of cash flow reporting and the differences that arise in contrast to the accrual based reporting used in the accounting records and the other financial statements.

In Chapter 3, the reporting of sales under the accrual method of accounting was illustrated. Sales are recorded by a company when the earnings process, i.e., the transfer of legal title to merchandise or the rendering of services is complete. In contrast, if sales were to be reported on a cash basis, the amount reported would simply be the sum of all cash received for goods and services in a particular period. For example, if the company sold merchandise totalling $50,000 with terms of $30,000 cash and the balance to be paid in 60 days, the Statement of Income for that one month period would report $50,000 in sales, while a cash flow reporting would show $30,000.

In a similar manner, accrual based accounting governs the recognition of expenses when the expense is incurred rather than when the cash is paid. As a result, if a company purchases $25,000 of merchandise and pays $10,000 cash and agrees to pay the remainder in 60 days, the Statement of Income for that month would show $25,000 in purchases, while cash flow reporting would show $10,000.

Another difference between cash flow reporting and accrual based reporting is the amount of expense recognized for accrual basis purposes that has NO cash flow impact. For example, each period that a company records depreciation expense, it reduces reported profits. However, the corresponding offset to such an expense is the Balance Sheet account of accumulated depreciation rather than cash or the promise of future cash flow. Thus the recording of this expense never impacts cash flow.

As a result of the examples shown above, an investor should now recognize that cash flow and net income are not usually equal amounts. Because investors may be more interested in cash flows, a common short-cut method used by many investors to determine cash flow is to take net income and add depreciation charges. This is not a good estimation technique because cash flow is impacted by many events, not simply the non-cash flow expenses.

For example, assume two companies report the same total sales for the period. A company whose sales are predominantly on credit with the resulting increase in Accounts Receivable may actually experience tight cash flow until the receivables are collected, while companies whose sales are for cash, may be able to exploit their market share due to their cash flow position. Yet both companies reported the same dollar value for sales. Thus it should be obvious that investors need to study the Statement of Cash Flows in addition to the Statement of Income accrual basis accounting. With this understanding, a description of the fundamentals of the Statement of Cash Flows should be more meaningful.

The Fundamentals of the Statement of Cash Flows

The Statement of Cash Flows is a relatively new financial statement and is required (beginning in 1988) in accordance with Financial Accounting Standard #95. As of this time, there is no other generally accepted title for this statement. The Statement of Cash Flows replaces the previously required Statement of Changes in Financial Position. Unlike that statement, the Statement of Cash Flows requires the use of cash basis reporting only.

The Statement of Cash Flows provides an investor with information on the actual cash inflow and outflow for the period. The "cash" designation in "cash flows" is important. Cash, for purposes of the Statement of Cash Flows, is designated as including cash and "cash equivalents." A cash equivalent is defined by FASB (Financial Accounting Standards Board) Standard #95 as "short-term, highly liquid investments." These investments are considered to be as liquid as cash if they are readily convertible to a specified amount of cash and have a short-term maturity, usually considered to be an original maturity of three months or less.

The statement requires that all cash flow activity be listed in one of three classifications: operating, investing or financing. Within each of these classifications, all cash activity—whether it is a cash inflow or a cash outflow—must be listed.

Cash flows classified as operating activity are the result of the company's normal business operations. For example, sales, payroll, advertising, interest expense and interest income are all considered operating activity for purposes of the Statement of Cash Flows. (You may remember that interest income and expense were classified as other revenue and expense on the Statement of Income.) Operating activities can also be identified as any transaction not classified as either an investing or financing transaction.

Perhaps the easiest way to understand events classified as investing activity, is to remember that if the transaction affects any of the company's long-term assets on the Balance Sheet, it is usually an investing activity. Investing activities are business transactions that involve investment by the company in their own productive resources or in the investment of other non-cash assets. Cash flow would also be affected by the sale of such productive resources or other non-cash assets. For example, the acquisition of plant and equipment, or the subsequent sale of a long-term investment in the common stock of another company, would classify as investing transactions for cash flow purposes.

Financing activities are transactions that involve the obtaining/repayment of the financial resources used to finance the company operations on a long-term basis. Such operations involve the issuing/repayment of debt, the sale of stock, the distribution of dividends and other creditor arrangements. Again, if one remembers that financing activities involve the "financing" of the company's operations either with debt or equity, it is easy to understand the nature of such a classification.

How and When Is a Statement of Cash Flows Prepared?

The Statement of Cash Flows reports the results of cash flow activity for a period of time, usually a month, a quarter or a year. Identical to the Statement of Income reporting, the Statement of Cash Flows is normally dated "for the period ended" on the last day of the accounting report period. If a company is issuing year-end statements, The Statement of Cash Flows will be dated "for the year ended December 31, 19XX."

The information reported on the Statement of Cash Flows reflects the sum of the transactions affecting each of the three designated business activities during the reporting period. Once again, this is in contrast to the Balance Sheet, which reports financial information as of a specific date with relevance only on that day.

The Statement of Cash Flows is usually prepared in conjunction with the other financial statements several days after the reporting period has ended. Preparation is usually on a monthly basis for distribution to the company's operating managers while publication to those outside of the company is once again limited to quarterly or year-end data.

In a manner similar to the Balance Sheet preparation, the Statement of Cash Flows has standard requirements governing presentation, format and other disclosure requirements. These standards are specified in Standard #95 and will be discussed in detail later in this chapter. Although there is minimal flexibility in the Statement of Cash Flows, Standard #95 allows a choice concerning the presentation of the cash flow from operating activity. The two allowable methods are known as the direct and indirect method, with Standard # 95 strongly recommending the direct method. Regardless of the method, both the direct and indirect method will produce the same amount of net cash flow from operating activities.

The direct method, also known as the gross method, actually details the gross receipts and the gross expenses on a cash basis for the operating period. In contrast, the indirect or net method as illustrated in Appendix 1 uses the net income reported on the Statement of Income as its starting figure. Adjustments are then added/subtracted to net income to effectively translate net income into the net cash flow from operating activities. These adjustments are discussed in detail later in this chapter.

Although the Financial Accounting Standards Board strongly recommended the use of the direct method, information available to date indicates that most companies strongly favor the indirect method. In a survey of 110 companies reported in the 1988 edition of Accounting Trends and Techniques compiled by the AICPA, 105 of the companies reported cash flow from operating activity on the indirect method. It is important to remember that regardless of the method, the net cash flow from operating activities will be the same.

How Does an Investor Use a Statement of Cash Flows?

An investor must consider both the amount and type of cash flow activity. Although net income is reported on the Statement of Income on an accrual basis, cash—not net income—is available to a company for use as payment of their financial obligations, i.e., income doesn't pay the bills—only cash can satisfy most debt obligations. As a result, cash flow information becomes critical in an investor's analysis of a company.

Key information found on the Statement of Cash Flows, combined with the notes to the financial statements (See Chapter 6 for additional information on note disclosures), provides answers to questions often asked by investors. The key questions investors need to consider are:

(1) What is the primary source of cash inflows, i.e., operations, financing or investing activities?
(2) Is the cash inflow sufficient to cover the amount of cash outflow?
(3) What are the primary activities requiring cash outflow?
(4) Do primary operations significantly contribute to the generation of cash inflows?
(5) Is the company providing cash to maintain the appropriate level of investment in the company's resources?
(6) What is the source of the company's borrowings?
(7) Is there sufficient cash to cover their debt obligations—both repayment and servicing of debt?
(8) Was sufficient cash available to pay the dividends that were declared?
(9) How does net income reconcile to cash flow provided or used in operations?
(10) What are the implications of the historical Cash Flow Statement for future cash flows?

To answer the above questions, an investor must thoroughly understand the Statement of Cash Flows. Throughout the following discussion it is important for the reader to continually refer to an actual Statement of Cash Flows, as shown in Appendix 1. Since the statement is comprised of three main sections, operating, investing and financing activities, the following pages will discuss each of these sections separately. This information will be followed by a discussion of the implications of each of these elements from an investor's perspective.

The breakdown of the cash flow information into the three sections aides an investor in a significant way since it highlights the companies activity according to specified categories of transactions. For example, if a company shows extensive use of long-term financing techniques to maintain their current operations, this would be evident in a Statement of Cash Flows and would certainly be of major concern to an investor.

Although the following discussion may seem to be of a technical accounting nature, it is important for investors to understand the details of the Statement of Cash Flows. In the financial statement package, it is the Statement of Cash Flows that provides the information most needed by investors, i.e., clear identification of the cash flow generated and how the cash proceeds are being used. In addition, this statement is now required as part of a company's financial reporting package and it represents that only cash-basis prepared statement.

Operating Activities

Operating activities are defined by Standard #95 as those transactions which do not meet the definition of investing or financing activities. Another, common sense approach, is to consider operating activity as the cash flow resulting from the main business activity reported on the Statement of Income, i.e., a "cash flow" version of a Statement of Income.

The most common operating transactions are those dealing with sales, cost of goods sold, payroll, advertising, maintenance & repairs, etc. However, for purposes of the Statement of Cash Flows, certain incidental transactions are considered operating activity, notably interest income, dividend income and interest expense.

It is important to realize however, that all items reported on the Statement of Income do not affect cash flows. Common examples of such items are depreciation and amortization, restructuring costs and deferred taxes (all are shown in the Appendix 1 operating section of the Statement of Cash Flows.) In addition, the gains and losses reported on the Statement of Income need to be adjusted so that the full impact of the transaction that caused the gain or loss can be reflected in the appropriate portion of the Statement of Cash Flows, i.e., financing or investing.

To illustrate, a gain on the disposal of assets was realized and cash proceeds were received from the sale. For cash flow purposes, the sale transaction would be considered a cash inflow from an investing activity.

As such, the gross proceeds from the sale would be reported in the investing section of the statement. (See "Proceeds from Sales of Property" $10,676 in the Appendix 1 Statement of Cash Flows.) To preclude a double reporting of the gain on the Statement of Cash Flow the portion of the transaction reported as a gain ($6,431—see Appendix 1) would have to be shown as a reduction from the net income on the Statement of Cash Flows to properly classify the amount of cash flows generated from operating activity.

The operating activity portion of the Statement of Cash Flows, prepared on an indirect method, begins with the net income reported on the Statement of Income. If there is an extraordinary item reported on the Statement of Income, an extraordinary gain must be subtracted, or in the case of an extraordinary loss the amount must be added back to net income, to arrive at Income before extraordinary items. This is consistent with the specialized treatment that extraordinary items receive on the Statement of Income.

The overall objective of the operating activity section, prepared under the indirect method, is to reconcile the reported accrual based net income figure to the cash flows generated from such activity. Beginning with the reported net income figure (or income before extraordinary items if such items exist) adjustments to that number must be made to reflect one of three possible items: (All of these adjustments can be seen by examining the Statement of Cash Flows in Appendix 1.)

(1) income/expense items that do not affect cash flow (e.g., depreciation and amortization, restructuring costs and deferred taxes previously identified)

(2) gains and losses (other than extraordinary items) that were the result of an investing or financing transaction (discussed above)

(3) changes in current asset or current liability accounts, commonly known as working capital

If a non-cash expense or loss was reported on the Statement of Income, the amount must be added back to the net income figure since it was initially subtracted in determining net income. If there is a revenue or gain reported, the amount must be subtracted from the net income figure since it was initially added in determining net income. Further adjustments are required for the working capital items. These items are usually the current asset and current liability accounts that are the result of operating activity. The most common accounts are receivables, inventories, payables, taxes, and accrued payroll.

If a working capital asset account increased from one period to the next, the net change in the account is subtracted from the net income figure to arrive at net cash flows provided by operations. It is easiest to understand this process if one examines accounts receivable. An increase in accounts receivable is caused by extending credit sales, a decrease is caused by cash collections. If the net change in the account was an increase, it simply means that the credit sales were in excess of cash collections for the period. If the objective is to effectively adjust net income for the credit sales made which did not yield cash collections, the amount must be subtracted since credit sales reported were higher than cash collections made.

However, the inverse is also true, i.e., if the account balance decreased from one period to the next, it means that the cash collections were in excess of the accrual-based sales reported for the year. In order to reflect the higher cash based sales, the net change in receivables must be added. In Appendix 1, examination of the Balance Sheet indicates a decrease in trade receivables. Thus, the net decrease in the receivable balance was added to net income on the Statement of Cash Flows.

For working capital liability accounts, a net increase in the account balance is added, while a net decrease would be subtracted. To illustrate, if the accrued payroll account increased from one period to the next, it means that the expense incurred and recorded on the Statement of Income is in excess of the actual cash payments made. Since a higher amount was subtracted from revenue in order to determine net income, it is necessary to add back the net increase in the liability account in order to properly state the lower amount of cash outflow from operations.

For a simplified example, assume salary expense on a Statement of Income of $35,000 and a salary payable account on the Balance Sheet with a beginning balance of $12,000 and an ending balance of $14,000. The reported net income figure was determined after subtracting accrual-based costs of $35,000, yet an increase in the salary payable account dictates that not all of the current period expense (i.e., $35,000) has been paid. Therefore, the $2,000 increase in the payable must be added back to net income to properly state the true cash-flow impact of salaries.

After adjustments have been made to the reported net income figure, the net cash provided, or in some cases net cash used, by operations is clearly identified.

The Investor's View of Operating Activity

A key question answered by analyzing the operating activity is the recognition of the difference between accrual based net income and cash flow, as well as providing the details which reconcile that difference. Once again, it is important for investors to know that a company is able to meet its financial obligations since only cash flow can satisfy financial obligations. Cash flows provided from operating activity indicates a positive situation for a company, while net cash consumed may indicate a potential negative situation from an investor's perspective.

Investors are concerned with capital growth of an investment. Capital growth can only occur if the company is perceived as an on-going, viable operation. One indication of a company's viability is their ability to support growth from cash flow generated by operating activity. In other words, cash flow from operations must be able to support all other business activities over the long-term. An investor is also concerned with a company's ability to pay dividends. Ideally, these dividends should be supported by the cash flow generated from the primary business, i.e., operations.

Investing Activities

The investing section reports all cash inflows and all cash outflows from activities that represent a company's investment in its long-term asset base. Among transactions that would be included in this section are the acquisition or sale of plant and equipment, the acquisition or sale of long-term investments, and the acquisition or sale of other long-term assets.

It is important to note, however, that Standard #95 does not allow the offset of cash inflows/outflows for related activities. For example, capital expenditures for acquisition of a new plant and equipment may not be netted against the cash proceeds generated from the sale of the old plant and equipment. This can easily be seen in the Appendix 1 Statement of Cash Flows where the reporting company shows gross outflows for property acquisition of $100,479 while indicating cash inflow from the sale of property in the amount of $10,676. This type of information enables the investor to easily identify how the long-term assets are being utilized.

The Investor's View of Investing Activities

The investing activity section of the Statement of Cash Flows is important in an investor's assessment of a company's physical operations. It is in this section that investors can determine the amount of cash committed in a given year to the acquisition of such long-term necessities as plant and equipment. A company who does not make a commitment by replacing plant and equipment may very well lose their competitive edge, thus not representing a wise investment. In addition, a large sale of plant and equipment may indicate a permanent reduction in productive capacity for the firm. Such information is also relevant to an investor.

Another item of significance reported in the investing section is a company's attempt at diversification or disinvestment of other business operations. For example, if a company sells an existing line of business, or acquires a business in a different market from which the company now operates, it indicates the company's operating and business philosophy to the investor. Thus the investor can seek additional information and make a more informed investment decision.

If a company is committed to maintaining their long-term asset base and therefore their long-term operating viability, it can be expected that the net cash activity for investing transactions most likely will be cash outflows that exceed cash inflows. This should not alarm an investor; once again it illustrates the need for a company to generate cash flow from operations in order to ultimately support all other business activities.

Financing Activities

The financing section of the Statement of Cash Flows reports all cash inflows and all cash outflows from activities which are the direct result of a company's financing decisions. Among transactions that would be included in this section are the issuance or reacquisition of stock, the issuance or repayment of bonds, pension financing, lease financing, revolving credit arrangements or any other debt acquisition or repayment of terms. In addition, the dividends paid to shareholders are reflected in this section. (Remember however, that the cost of servicing the debt agreements, i.e., interest payments, are shown as an operating activity.)

Once again, the activity reported in this section does not allow for the offset of cash inflows/outflows for related activities. In the Statement of Cash Flows in Appendix 1, the repayment of long-term debt is reported at $166,613 while the proceeds from issuing new long-term debt is $254,828. Requiring these two financing transactions to be reported separately provides investors with a clearer picture of the company's financing decisions.

The Investors's View of Financing Activities

The financing section of the Statement of Cash Flows is critical to an investors assessment of the financial health of the organization. Although an investor can also examine the Balance Sheet for such information via the balances in the asset and liability accounts, the Statement of Cash Flows identifies the source of the cash and how it was subsequently disbursed. It is in this section that an investor can see the effects of a company's financing decisions, i.e., what was borrowed, what was repaid, what amount of dividends were paid, and whether there were funds provided by additional stockholder contributions or funds used to reacquire their own stock.

Simply stated, if cash inflows exceed cash outflows, the company borrowed more than it repaid; if cash outflows exceeded cash inflows, they repaid more than they borrowed. From an investors perspective, both situations need further examination. For example, if cash outflows exceed cash inflows, it may appear that the company did not have the need to borrow funds and were in fact repaying previous debts. However, an investor must look at that situation in conjunction with the investing portion of the statement. If no additional funds were borrowed and yet investment in plant and equipment is needed, funds either have to come from operating activity or financing activity. It may be that the company decided to repay existing debts rather than invest in plant and equipment. Obviously, such a decision has ramifications for an investor who must consider both the short-term and the long-term perspectives.

In addition, cash inflows reported in this portion of the Statement of Cash Flows must be examined in conjunction with the operating section of the statement. If cash provided from financing activities represents the majority of cash inflow for the company, compounded perhaps by the need for investment in plant and equipment, an investor must consider the viability of the company.

Thus it is necessary for an investor to examine each of the three sections of the Statement of Cash Flows—operating, investing, and financing—both individually as well as collectively, in order to make an appropriate assessment of the company's cash flow. Since an investor will use cash flow in conjunction with their earnings assessment as an indicator of future potential for the company, the information contained in the Statement of Cash Flows is critical.

Other Statement of Cash Flow Information

After the sections on operating, investing, and financing activity are listed, Standard # 95 also requires that certain other financial information be reported. If the company has foreign currency exchange transactions, the cash effect of the exchange rates on foreign currency accounts must be shown on the Statement of Cash Flows.

After foreign exchange account information is listed, the Statement of Cash Flows must report the reconcilement between the net change in the cash and cash equivalent accounts listed on the Balance Sheet with the net cash provided or used from the operating, investing, and financing transactions combined. This is shown on the statement by adding the net cash provided to or subtracting the net cash used from the beginning cash balance to arrive at the ending cash balance for the period.

In the section on operating activity, the non-cash impact of certain expenses was discussed. It is also possible that a company will have investing and financing transactions that do not affect cash flow. At first this may seem unusual, but with the creative financing and investing options currently available, these types of transaction may occur. Standard #95 does require that any type of non-cash transaction affecting financing or investing activity be reported in either a supplemental schedule or disclosed in the notes to the financial statements.

Additional disclosure requirements specified by Standard #95 involve reporting information on the company policy of determining which items are classified as cash equivalents and the amount of cash paid for interest and income taxes. In addition, if the statement reports operating activity using the direct method, the changes in receivables, inventory, and payables must be identified as well as a reconciliation of net income to net cash flow from operating activity.

Examining the above disclosure requirements for operating activity, coupled with the difficulty of preparing the operating activity results on a direct method, provide some insight on why the majority of companies chose to prepare the operating section information under the indirect method.

Limitations of Cash Flow Information

Because of its relative newness, it is actually difficult to identify the limitations of this statement. In addition, unlike the other financial statements whose limitations are somewhat universally accepted, the limitations of cash flow information may depend upon one's perspective. From an investor's perspective, the Statement of Cash Flows represents a substantial improvement over the funds based Statement of Changes in

Financial Position since cash flow information provides a critical data base. However, the statement is once again a historical statement that provides a record of past events. Since investors are often trying to make decisions about a company's future earnings and cash flow, the record of past cash flow has inherent limitations.

Another perceived limitation to such a statement is its cash-based reporting in contrast to the accrual based approach of the remaining three financial statements. However, the Statement of Cash Flows is linked to the Statement of Income via the net income amount and The Balance Sheet via the reported cash balances for the beginning and end of the period. (See Appendix 2)

The fourth and final financial statement, the Statement of Changes in Shareholder Equity, does not impact the Statement of Cash Flows. However, in a manner similar to The Statement of Cash Flows, the Statement of Changes in Shareholder Equity also serves as a link between the Statement of Income and the Balance Sheet and is graphically illustrated in Appendix 2. This link is important to remember as the Statement of Changes in Shareholder Equity is described in detail in Chapter 5.

CHAPTER 5

THE STATEMENT OF CHANGES IN SHAREHOLDER EQUITY

The Statement of Changes in Shareholder Equity is the fourth financial statement included in the reporting package. This statement reports the account balances, as well as the details of the changes, in each of the owner's equity accounts. There does not appear to be a great deal of title uniformity in this statement; as a result, the information is reported under a variety of names. Other commonly noted titles for this statement are The Statement of Changes in Shareholder Investment, The Statement of Changes in Stockholder's Equity, The Statement of Stockholder's Equity, and the Statement of Shareholder's Equity.

The most descriptive titles are those that contain the phrase Statement of Changes in.... since change is what the statement portrays, i.e., the detailed information on the changes in the shareholder equity accounts from period to period. However, with the apparent movement in recent years to present limited shareholder account information on the Balance Sheet, the Statement of Changes in Shareholder Equity also provides investors with basic information concerning the equity components of a company.

Changes in Shareholder Equity Basics

The Statement of Changes in Shareholder Equity provides investors with information on the equity structure of the company as well as the changes in that structure since the last reporting period. Although accounting theory considers equity to be comprised of several sub-categories—contributed capital, earned capital and other capital—published financial statements do not normally make such a distinction between the different types of equity.

Specific equity account balances are occasionally listed in the shareholder equity section of the Balance Sheet. (See The Balance Sheet in Appendix 1.) In contrast, some companies only identify total stockholder's' equity without identifying the specific details of those accounts and their respective balances. Thus, an investor must closely examine the Statement of Changes in Shareholder Equity to obtain the basic information on such accounts.

Information on the account balances for stock, additional contributed capital, treasury stock, retained earnings, foreign currency translation adjustments, and any other equity accounts can be found on the Statement of Changes in Shareholder Equity. In addition, the detailed information supporting these account balances can also be found on the statement. Details such as the type of stock(s), the amount of stock authorized, issued or outstanding, the amount of additional capital contributed through the sale of stock, as well as treasury stock information is usually readily available.

Current period transactions affecting these accounts will also appear on the Statement of Changes in Shareholder Equity. Examples of such transactions are the issuance of stock, the temporary reacquisition or permanent retirement of stock, the additional contributed capital received from stock transactions, the reinvestment of current period earnings, dividends declared by the board of directors, and the impact of foreign currency translation adjustments. (See the Statement of Changes in Shareholder Equity in Appendix 1.)

How and When Is the Statement of Changes in Shareholder Equity Prepared?

The Statement of Changes in Shareholder Equity reports the results of equity transactions for a period of time, usually a month, quarter or year. As an externally published statement, the Statement of Changes in Shareholder Equity usually is found only on a quarterly or yearly basis. Identical to the reporting of income and cash flows, the Statement of Changes in Shareholder Equity is normally dated for the period ended on the last day of the accounting period. If the company is issuing year-end statements, the Statement of Changes in Shareholder Equity will be dated "for the year ended June 30 19XX."

The information reported on the Statement of Changes in Shareholder Equity reflects the sum of the transactions affecting each of the equity accounts. Once again, the account balances of each equity account may or may not be found on the Balance Sheet, but both the account balances and the account activity can be found in the Statement of Changes in Shareholder Equity. The information affecting each of the equity accounts is normally presented for three consecutive years, the same time period illustrated in the Statement of Income presentation.

The Statement of Changes in Shareholder Equity is usually prepared in conjunction with the other financial statements several days after the reporting period has ended. However, given the nature of the information reported on this statement, it does not usually receive the same distribution that the other financial statements do. The limited distribution can be considered a function of the type of information presented in such a statement, i.e., the information is of limited value for operating managers but is appropriate for high level management, investors or potential investors, bankers and other creditors.

An interesting point to note is that while the Statement of Changes in Shareholder Equity can be found as a fourth financial statement accompanying the other financial statements, some companies do not publish this statement other than as a footnote to the financial statements. Although the information and structure of the presentation is the same, the location of the information within the context of the annual report package can differ. Because present accounting and reporting requirements do not prohibit such a presentation mechanism, an investor should look in the notes to the financial statements if they cannot locate the Statement of Changes in Shareholder Equity with the other financial statements.

How Does an Investor Use the Statement of Changes in Shareholder Equity?

The Statement of Changes in Shareholder Equity provides information on the existing equity structure of a company. Since an investor's commitment is part of that equity, the information contained in the statement is of major interest. As an investor contemplating a change in his existing investment or as a potential investor evaluating a company, the information portrayed in this statement should be thoroughly understood and analyzed.

Key information found on the Statement of Changes in Shareholder Equity, combined with the notes to the financial statements (see Chapter 6 for additional information on note disclosures), provides answers to questions often asked by investors. Such key questions are as follows:

(1) What is the equity structure of the company?
(2) What stock has been authorized?
(3) What stocks are issued and outstanding?
(4) How much additional stock has been issued and why?
(5) What is the requirement for preferred dividends?
(6) Is there treasury stock—if so, what is the amount and why was it reacquired?
(7) Have dividends been consistently declared?

(8)   What restrictions on dividend declarations exist?
(9)   Are there any appropriations or restrictions on retained earnings?
(10) Have the changes in any of the equity accounts been due to unusual circumstances?

To answer many of the above questions, an investor must thoroughly understand the nature of each equity element, the cause of any increase or decrease in the account, and the implications of such changes. Since the structure and format of The Statement of Changes in Shareholder Equity varies in presentation but contains the same primary elements from company to company, the following discussion will focus on the specific equity accounts found within most companies. The discussion will then focus on the investor's view of these accounts.

Equity Terminology

Before additional discussion continues, basic terminology related to both preferred and common stock must be considered. Par value is nothing more than an amount assigned to any stock (preferred or common) by the corporation within the limits of the incorporating state. Depending upon the state, such a value is considered to represent "legal capital." Par value does not have any relationship to the market value of a stock (unlike bonds where par value has some economic significance) nor to its book value; it is simply an accounting tool used to assign a dollar value to the individual stock account. Amounts received in excess of the par value are recorded in the additional paid-in capital account (to be discussed later.)

For example, a company's corporate charter may have authorized 250,000 shares of $5 par value common stock and the company issued 50,000 of those shares at $8. Thus the "legal capital" is represented by 50,000 shares times $5 or $250,000 shown in the common stock account while the excess of the market price over the par value of $3 per share ($150,000) represents additional paid-in capital.

Stock may also be recorded at a stated value which is the same as par value for financial statement purposes. A third option is no-par stock, which is more commonly issued as common stock. No-par stock simply does not assign a value to the face of the stock and any proceeds received from the sale of such stock are recorded as the value of the stock. Using the previous example, assume that the stock was issued as no-par stock and sold for $8. Thus the common stock account in this situation would contained $400,000.

Other terminology which an investor needs to understand is the difference between authorized, issued and outstanding shares. Once again, these terms apply both to preferred and common stock. Authorized stock is the number of shares a corporation can legally issue consistent with the company's corporate charter. In the previous example, the authorized stock totaled 250,000 shares. Issued shares are the shares of stock initially sold to a shareholder. Outstanding stocks are shares that have been issued and are still in the hands of a shareholder (in the example, 50,000 shares were issued and at present are still in the hands of the shareholders.)

Treasury stock shares are those that have been issued but have been reacquired by the company and are no longer owned by a shareholder. For example, assume the company repurchased 10,000 of the 50,000 shares on the open market at $10 a share. Although the issued shares remain at 50,000 (with the corresponding $250,000 in the stock account), the issued and outstanding shares are thus reduced to a total of 40,000 and the treasury stock account would reflect the 10,000 shares and $100,000. It is important to note that the temporary reacquisition of stock does not impact the common stock account but is reflected in the treasury stock account which represents a reduction of the total equity of the company.

Preferred Stock

Preferred Stock is the first account found within the owner's equity section of the Balance Sheet and The Statement of Changes in Shareholder Equity. The account is listed first since it represents the most permanent of the equity accounts. Permanent in this sense refers to the accounts and how they are affected in the event of liquidation. The losses of liquidation impact the corporate equity reporting structure from the "bottom up," i.e., from the least permanent accounts (common stock) to the most permanent accounts (preferred stock.) Thus, in liquidation the losses are absorbed by the common stockholders before the preferred stockholders. Therefore, preferred stock is listed first (the most permanent) in the order of reporting the equity accounts because it is affected only after all of the remaining corporate equity accounts have absorbed the negative impact of liquidation.

It is important for an investor to realize that when one talks about investments in stocks and bonds and the impact of liquidation on those investments, bondholders are considered creditors of a corporation while those holding common or preferred stock are equity investors. Thus in the event of liquidation, an investor has more protection as a bondholder with creditor status than an equity investor in preferred or common stock.

However, investment in preferred stock provides more protection in the event of liquidation than does investment in common.

The dollar value assigned to the Preferred Stock account is the par value or stated value of the stock times the number of shares issued for each type of Preferred Stock authorized. It is not uncommon for a corporation to have several different types of preferred stock, varying mostly in the amount of stated dividend rates. Increases in the preferred stock account(s) are caused by additional stock issuances and decreases are caused by retirement or conversion of the stock(s) to common. However, there is additional information for an investor to consider when evaluating preferred stock.

Why would an investor want to invest in Preferred Stock, or conversely what does the existing issue of Preferred Stock mean to a potential investor. Preferred stock means exactly as its title suggests, i.e., it is stock that receives preferential treatment. As mentioned earlier, one of the ways in which preferred stock is preferred is in the event of liquidation. However, a more notable preference is the stock dividend preference, i.e., preferred stockholders are entitled to a stated dividend rate and are guaranteed to receive their dividend prior to the common stockholders. The stated rate is normally expressed as a percentage of par or stated value, or as a fixed dollar value for no-par stock. As a result of issuing preferred stock, the corporation has implicitly made a commitment of funds/cash to satisfy the dividend obligation for preferred stockholders before anything may be paid to common stockholders. It is important to note that preferred stock does not commit the corporation to declaring a dividend; it does commit the corporation to a specified dollar value of dividends for preferred stockholders if they choose to declare a dividend.

In addition, preferred stock may contain other attractive features. One feature, known as cumulative, allows the dividends that are undeclared to accumulate over the years so that when the corporation declares a current year dividend, each of the past years dividends must also be paid. Thus, even if a dividend is not declared every year, the cumulative preferred stockholder may ultimately receive those undeclared dividends (unless a corporate reorganization prevents such action.) Needless to say, this is an attractive feature for preferred stock.

Another possibility for preferred stock is the participating feature, which allows the stockholder to share in the excess dividends a company may declare. Without this feature, a preferred stockholder is locked into the dividend rate stated on the face of the stock. As a result, if the company has an extremely good year, preferred stockholders may not receive any corresponding benefit unless the preferred stock has the participating feature. However, there are not many companies who issue participating preferred stock.

A company can also issue convertible preferred stock. This feature gives the preferred stockholder the option to convert the preferred stock to common stock at the holders discretion. As a result, preferred stockholders may want to convert their preferred to common if the common stock becomes a more attractive investment.

The Investor's View of Preferred Stock

What do all the options and stipulations of preferred stock mean to an investor? Primarily, an investor is guaranteed a stated dividend rate if the dividends are declared by the company. However, the inverse is that the company must maintain the cash flow to support the dividend requirement. Depending upon the company's cash flow position, this requirement may represent a drain on resources that are needed in other areas. One can counter that preferred stock guarantees a dividend rate, not necessarily a dividend. This is true, however, the market value of the stock may be adversely affected in the event that the company must use its resources for items other than dividends.

An additional consideration for investors are the possible features preferred stock offers over an investment in common stock. The cumulative feature offsets the possibility of a dividend not being declared in a given year, and the participating feature offers an investor the possibility of additional dividends above the minimum guaranteed rate. However, if interest rates rise after the investment, the value of the preferred will fall. Thus there is also some downside risk an investor must consider. An additional consideration for the preferred stockholders is that they will often give up their voting rights in the management of the company. However, return on investment rather than voting rights may be of prime concern.

Common Stock

Common stock is the next account listed in the equity section of the Balance Sheet and the Statement of Changes in Shareholder's Equity and is the stock most often issued by corporations. Once again, a corporation may have multiple types of common stock, usually distinguished by par value stock, no-par stock and stated value stock. A corporation may also offer different classes of common stock; for example, one class may be eligible to receive cash dividends while another class may not.

Unlike Preferred stock however, there are not many options and features available to common stockholders. Common stock does not receive the preferential dividend treatment offered to preferred stockholders nor does it receive the liquidation preference.

The dollar value assigned to the Common Stock account is the par or stated value times the number of shares issued. In the event of no-par common stock, the dollar value in the account represents the total proceeds received at the time of the stock issuance. Increases in the account are caused by new stock issuances; decreases in the account are caused by permanent retirement of stock. Newly issued stock can be the result of a totally new stock issuance or a sale of previously authorized, yet unissued stock. It can also be the result of a stock dividend or a stock split. The Statement of Changes in Shareholder Equity discloses the issuance of stock and often notes why it was issued, i.e., for stock option plans, employee savings plans, stock conversions, stock splits or stock dividends or sale to investors to raise additional capital.

It is important to note that a company's temporary reacquisition of its own common stock does not affect the common stock account. That type of transaction is recorded in a treasury stock account which will be discussed later in this chapter.

An Investor's View of Common Stock

Investors must contrast investment in Common Stock with investment in Preferred Stock; this is largely a function of an individual's investment philosophy. Although wide variety of features and options are available to preferred stockholders and not available to common stockholders, it is usually the growth potential that makes common stock a potentially lucrative investment. For example, common stockholders can share in the profitable periods of a company via increased dividends declared by the board. Unless an investor has participating preferred stock, only common stockholders have the ability to gain increased dividends when a company experiences an unusually profitable year. However, a common stock holder can also share in the unprofitable periods as evidenced by the reduction in the dividend rate during non-profitable periods. Preferred stockholders are protected in such an event, particularly if they hold cumulative preferred stock.

Another consideration is that Common Stock represents true ownership in a company as evidenced by the voting rights conferred with the stock. While many investors do not exercise these voting privileges and in reality have no interest in doing so, the ability to register their displeasure with company policies or procedures does in fact exist. In contrast, many preferred stockholders do not have such options available.

In addition, investors must view their investment in common stock relative to the amount of stock presently outstanding. Increases in the number of shares of stock outstanding requires a greater cash outlay for dividends that are declared. As a result, additional stock issuances increase a company's "cost" of declaring a dividend, or it may actually decrease the amount of dividends received per share when only a limited amount of funds are available for dividend distribution. In contrast, additional funds raised with the issuance of additional shares can finance the growth of a company thereby leading to increased dividends and rising share values.

A further consideration for existing common stockholders is the position they hold relative to the other stockholders. When a company is considering a new stock issue, existing stockholders are sometimes granted the right to make stock acquisition prior to new investors in order that they may maintain their relative position of ownership within the company. If a stockholder owns 15% of the existing shares of stock, they are granted the right to purchase 15% of the new issuance in order to maintain their 15% ownership. Stock dividends and stock splits are normally structured in such a way that the dividend or split maintains the stockholder's relative ownership position.

Stock dividends and stock splits have similar and yet different effects on an investment. Both stock splits and stock dividends provide additional shares of stock to the investors and correspondingly require an investor to redistribute the cost basis of the stock. An advantage to the investors occurs only if the cash dividend rate per share of stock for subsequent dividends remains the same thus increasing their overall dividend received. If the dividend rate is cut to match the corresponding increase in shares, the stock split or dividend does not provide any additional benefit to the investor.

Potential investor's concerns are somewhat different from existing investor's concerns. A potential investor is looking for the continuation of, or the increase in, dividend payout. Past history on dividends declared can be found for the most recent three years in the Statement of Changes in Shareholder Equity. They are also concerned with the market appreciation that is expected to occur. However, little data can be obtained in the financial statements to help an investor with this type of information. A potential investor must also examine the Statement of Changes in Shareholder Equity for basic information on the type of equity issued by the company and judge how their investment in such a company will be affected by the existing structure.

Additional Paid-in Capital

Additional paid-in capital, also known as paid in excess of par is the third and last of the contributed equity components. The balance in this account reflects the dollars received by the corporation from stock issuances in excess of the par or stated value of the preferred or common stock. In the example earlier in this chapter, 50,000 shares of common stock with a par value of $5 were issued at a market price of $8. As a result, the additional paid-in capital account was increased by $3 per share or $150,000. (This account is obviously not affected by the issuance of no-par stock.)

From an investor's perspective, this account does not have any particular significance. Changes in this account occur when new stock is issued and when stock is permanently retired. This account can also be affected by treasury stock transactions.

Retained Earnings

Retained earnings is the net of profits, losses, dividends and prior period adjustments over the life of the company. It is considered an "earned" capital account, in contrast to the stock or "contributed" capital accounts and thus appears after the stock accounts on the Balance Sheet and The Statement of Changes in Shareholder Equity.

The typical changes in this account are increases for the current year's net income reported on the Statement of Income (or decreases in the event of a net loss for the period); decreases for dividends declared in the current year; and increases or decreases for prior period adjustments necessary due to accounting error corrections.

An Investor's View of Retained Earnings

From an investor's viewpoint, retained earnings represents a company's willingness to reinvest in the business. If a company is not willing to do so, it may represent a poor investment to an outside investor. However, a company must strike a balance between reinvestment in its company and the payment of dividends necessary to keep the stockholders satisfied.

Of particular concern to an investor is a decreasing retained earnings base since it indicates either a decrease in earnings or a company's willingness to pay dividends in excess of current period earnings. Both of these actions cause a decrease in the company's earned equity base. Although a company may in fact declare dividends in excess of its current period earnings, it cannot do so indefinitely or the earned capital base disappears, leaving only contributed capital. If this situation occurs, the potential long-term effects on a company can be negative. An investor is certainly interested in dividends but not to the exclusion of the overall financial health of a corporation.

Treasury Stock

Treasury Stock is listed within the equity section of the Balance Sheet and the Statement of Changes in Shareholder Equity, but it is actually a reduction of the firm's total shareholder equity. This account arises when a corporation repurchases its own stock on a temporary basis. A company reacquires its own stock for a wide variety of reasons, such as thwarting a take-over bid or manipulating the stock price, and can subsequently reissue the stock when it is considered prudent to do so.

The acquisition of treasury stock reduces the number of shares outstanding and therefore those shares are ineligible for dividend payment. However, treasury stock shares are not considered as a reduction of common shares issued since their reacquisition is temporary in nature.

The treasury stock account is increased with the reacquisition of the shares by the company and is reduced when those shares are reissued to investors. When purchasing treasury stock, most companies record the shares at cost, although the par-value method is also an option. At the point of reissuance, the excess of the selling price received over the cost assigned to the shares when originally reacquired is credited to the additional paid-in-capital account. In the event that the price received upon reissuance is less than the cost to reacquire, the additional paid-in-capital account is reduced. In the event that there is no balance in the additional paid-in-capital account, and the stock reissuance is below cost, the retained earnings account must be reduced.

In the previous example in the chapter, the company originally issued 50,000 shares and reacquired 10,000 shares on the open market at $10 per share. Thus the treasury stock account would reflect a balance of $100,000. If the company reissued the stock several months later at $12 per share, the treasury stock account would be reduced to zero and the additional paid-in-capital account would be increased for the excess

($2/share) of the reissue price times the number of shares (a total of $20,000) over the company's initial cost of repurchasing the stock ($10/share.)

The Investor's View of Treasury Stock

An investor's logical question concerning treasury stock is "why did the company reacquire its own stock?" Unfortunately, this item of information is not usually found in the financial statements. A corollary question is whether the funds used to reacquire the stock represented an appropriate use of cash and whether competing demands for the company's resources could be satisfied from other sources.

Dividends are always of interest to investors. Since treasury stocks shares are ineligible for dividends, an investor must consider those shares when evaluating the cash demands required of a corporation for dividend declaration and payment. Conversely, the subsequent reissuance of those shares will cause an increase in the cash required for dividends.

Additional information shown on the Statement of Changes in Shareholder Equity is the subsequent reissuance of stock from the treasury. Reissuance is often used to satisfy the requirements of employee savings plans and employee stock ownership plans.

Foreign Currency Translation Adjustment

The last item normally found in the Statement of Changes in Shareholder Equity is an adjustment to the equity balance due to foreign currency translations required by the Financial Accounting Standards Board Statement #52. The adjustment is the result of the translation of the financial statements of foreign operations whose primary financial information was recorded in their local operating currency. These adjustments remain as part of the equity section until the foreign operation is sold. Due to the nature of this account, there is limited information available to an investor.

Other Considerations and Limitations in Shareholder Equity Reporting

It is important for investors to examine the equity portion of the Balance Sheet in conjunction with the Statement of Changes in Shareholder Equity. In doing so, an investor can obtain the best available information concerning both the equity structure and equity transactions during the period. Further information can also be obtained from an in-depth reading of the note disclosures.

Of concern to an investor is the limited amount of information on shareholder equity transactions and the basis for making such a transaction. For example, the reacquisition of treasury stock and the reasons justifying that transaction cannot be found in the financial statement. In addition, there is virtually no information available on the foreign currency translations adjustments other than the dollar amount listed.

A further limitation is that the Statement of Changes in Shareholder Equity must be examined in conjunction with the equity portion of the Balance Sheet in order to get the complete picture of the equity activity. A significant limitation of equity reporting is the lack of standardization among the published statements. For example, a company may only report the total equity balances on the Balance Sheet, while the Statement of Changes in Shareholder Equity report the changes in the account balances. Information on the number of shares authorized and issued as well as the par value or stated value of the stock sometimes appears in the equity section of the Balance Sheet while other companies report such information as part of the Statement of Changes in Shareholder Equity; yet, another might report such information at the bottom of the statement. The lack of uniformity in presentation can hamper an investor's ability to analyze the information.

Because investor's are often aided by the note disclosure to the financial statements, an entire chapter, Chapter 6, has been devoted to this topic.

FINANCIAL STATEMENT
FOOTNOTE DISCLOSURES

The financial statement footnote disclosures are a significant part of the financial statement package. However, they are often overlooked by investors who read and analyze financial statement data. Technically these disclosures are referred to as footnote disclosures or disclosure notes, but most companies simply identify them as "notes to the financial statements."

The amount and type of information contained in the note disclosures enhances a company's ability to report operating and financial results. Proper utilization of such data will greatly aid an investor in evaluating a company's financial operations.

Note Disclosure Basics

Assume an investor receives a recommendation to buy a particular company's stock due to its increased net income and earnings per share in the current year. Although the reported increase in earnings appears attractive, further examination of the financial statement information, particularly the note disclosures, might indicate that the increase in earnings was due to a one-time gain on early debt extinguishment. Elimination of that gain from the reported earnings actually results in a decrease in actual operating earnings. Thus, the key information found in the note disclosures provides answers to complex questions often asked by investors.

Individual questions on the nature of financial statement elements will be discussed in the following pages. However, investors often have questions on the use of note disclosures. These questions can be identified as follows:

(1) How do the note disclosures supplement the information contained in the financial statements?

(2) Is the note disclosure consistent with the information contained in the financial statements?

(3)   How can this information be used to better understand the financial position of a company?

(4)   How can note information aid in making an intelligent investment decision?

(5)   What are the elements identified in the note disclosures that have not yet been recorded in the financial statements?

(6)   What impact will these events have on the present and future financial position of the company?

The note disclosures provide investors with a great deal of financial information and are designed to supplement the numbers reported in the financial statements (discussed in the previous four chapters). Some of the note disclosures provide data which can be considered general information, such as, a description of accounting policies used by the company. Other note disclosures provide detailed information on specifics such as lease agreements, taxes or debt arrangements. Several note disclosures are specifically required by accounting regulations, while other data is provided by the company to aid in the understanding of its financial information.

Importance of Footnotes

One might question why preparation of such note disclosures is necessary. First and foremost, any company that is publicly held is required to present the note disclosure information in accordance with SEC reporting requirements. However, in order to understand the importance of such a requirement, one must realize that the overriding goal of financial information is summarized in an accounting principle known as "full-disclosure." This principle is critical because it means that an investor should receive all information that is necessary or relevant to make an informed investing decision. Although this does not guarantee a 100% complete data base, it insures that certain financial and operating is information available to investors.

Because not all financial information lends itself to the dollars and cents reporting format found in the financial statements, the note disclosures can report such data while providing background information on the financial events. In addition, note disclosures provide support for the numbers reported within the financial statements. A further benefit is the reporting of events that may have recently occurred, or may be about to happen, that would not usually be reported in the financial statements. This type of information is important for investors trying to accurately assess a company's financial position.

For example, assume a company is in the process of negotiating a sale of major assets which will permanently reduce the productive capacity. Since they are still in the negotiating stage and no formal commitments have been made, the potential sale of such assets would not be reflected in the financial statements since the sale has not yet occurred and no dollar value has been placed on the transaction. As an investor or potential investor in the company, knowledge of a pending reduction in permanent capacity may very well influence the investment decision, i.e., an investor may decide that the short-term impact of such a decision (for example, a loss on the disposal and a reduction of earnings) is more than offset by the beneficial long-term impact on total profitability. Under the full disclosure principle governing the reporting of financial information, the company would be required to disclose the negotiations in the note disclosures, particularly if such a transaction might have a significant impact on the company.

An additional benefit of note disclosures is their ability to integrate what may appear to be separate pieces of unrelated information. For example, a company's debt situation is of critical importance to an investor. The Balance Sheet reports the balance owed to the creditors at the end of the reporting period, the Statement of Income reports the amount of interest expense incurred in servicing the debt for the current period, and the Statement of Cash Flows reports any cash received or cash paid for acquiring or retiring debt during the same time period. However, each of these transactions is part of a larger issue, i.e., the debt of the company and the ramifications of having such debt. To illustrate, a company with an average debt ratio may actually be more risky if it has a large amount of debt maturities at a time when interest rates are high or market conditions are not receptive to additional debt issuances. The note disclosure dealing with long-term debt provides an investor with a more complete picture of the financial event. Information such as the amount of debt, the type of debt, the due date of the debt, and the interest rate incurred on such debt can be found in the note disclosure.

Criticisms of Note Disclosures

Although the advantages noted above are of prime consideration, there are some disadvantages associated with note disclosures. The most often cited problem is that they are difficult to read and understand. Although there are many who would agree with such a statement, it is important to realize that the notes are difficult to understand because of the nature of the transactions involved. Accounting and financing transactions have become increasingly complex during the recent decades and the complexity most likely will continue. While a company must try and simplify such complex events into financial information that can be read by investors, this is not necessarily an easy task to accomplish.

Another problem with footnote disclosures is that their preparation is required, yet they are often overlooked by investors who read financial statements. As a result, a great deal of information is "lost." Any investor who is willing to take the time to interpret the critical information contained in the notes will actually possess an advantage in the investment decision-making process.

A further criticism is that they provide "information overload," i.e., too much information depending upon the financial statement reader's requirements. However, the accounting regulatory agencies feel that it is better to err on the side of too much information rather than not enough information. From an investor's perspective, it would appear that having too much information would be preferable to having limited information; otherwise, it would be extremely difficult to make an intelligent investment decision.

A final disadvantage of note disclosures is that they may provide information on events which may subsequently not happen. In an earlier example, the potential sale of assets resulting in a permanent reduction in capacity was discussed. Obviously an investor would want to know about such an event when making the investment decision. However, if the negotiations were unsuccessful and no sale of the assets ultimately occurred, the investor's decision considered the possibility of an event that never occurred. Obviously, this type of reporting can create some problems for investors.

Considering the advantages and disadvantages discussed in the previous pages, it is important to remember that the overall usefulness of the note disclosures outweighs the negative aspects. The more information an investor has, the better the investment decision.

How and When Are Note Disclosures Prepared?

The note disclosures typically accompany published financial statements, usually in quarterly and annual reports. However, the note disclosures contained in quarterly reports are not standardized to the extent that the annual note disclosures are. As a result, the quarterly notes are not as consistently prepared, are usually much fewer in number, and provide less information than those in the annual report. Thus an investor should focus on the notes contained in the annual report.

How Does an Investor Use Financial Statement Note Disclosures?

Without note disclosures, the data base for considering investment options is incomplete and may result in a poor investment decision. Above all, note disclosures expand the information available and the interrelationships among financial elements reported in the financial statements, thus facilitating the examination of the "big picture."

The information contained in the note disclosures is grouped by type of financial transaction, i.e., debt, taxes, plant and equipment, pensions, etc. An investor will examine the components of the various financial statements together with the note disclosure, thus providing a complete picture of the related transactions. In the following pages, the common note disclosures will be discussed, emphasizing how the note is a mechanism for assimilating diverse pieces of financial information related to a common event. The discussion will then focus on the use of the information in the investment decision-making process.

Individual Note Disclosures

Summary of Significant Accounting Policies

The first footnote disclosure in the annual report is the summary of significant accounting policies. This note sets the stage for the financial processes used by a company in recording their accounting information and preparing their financial reports. Because various methods of generally accepted accounting and reporting alternatives are available, it is required that companies clearly identify the accounting method used in reporting their financial results. Interpretation of the accounting information within this context is critical in the understanding of the reported financial results.

For example, determining the cost basis of inventory allows a company to choose among several costing methods, typically first-in, first-out (FIFO), last-in, first-out (LIFO), average costing or specific identification. Companies must also choose from among various alternatives in the recording of the annual depreciation expense, which subsequently affects the reporting of property, plant and equipment. There are four methods of depreciation currently allowed under generally accepted accounting principles. Two of these methods are based on a uniform expensing over time (straight-line) and usage (units of production), and two of the methods are accelerated methods (sum of the years digits and double declining balance) which permit a faster write-off of the asset cost.

Another common disclosure in the summary of significant accounting policies is the principle of consolidation used by a parent company. This note identifies the subsidiaries of the parent company and discloses which results are reported in the consolidated financial statements and which results are reported using the equity method. A further disclosure of significant accounting policy must be made by a company identifying their definition of the term "cash equivalent" used in the reporting of cash flows. This requirement was new with the issuance of FASB Statement #95, which again permitted companies some choice in reporting cash flow information.

Other statements of accounting policy often noted are income taxes, foreign currency translation, accounting changes and other disclosures necessitated by industry specific accounting and reporting practices.

The Investor's View of Significant Accounting Policies

The disclosure of significant accounting policies is critical to an investor because it provides the background for interpreting the financial statement results. A proper reading and analysis of the financial statements cannot occur unless they are examined in light of the accounting policies and procedures used by the reporting company. Other companies, even within the same industry, may choose a different yet acceptable method of accounting for comparable transactions. Thus it becomes important to understand the policy statements when comparing information from different companies.

How should an investor use the summary of significant accounting policies when interpreting financial statement results? For example, if a company has selected and identified an accelerated method of depreciation, an investor would expect to see higher amount of depreciation expense reported in the early years of the asset life. Naturally as the asset ages, the reported depreciation will decline. As a result, higher depreciation reported on the Statement of Income in the early years will reduce reported profits and correspondingly cause a decrease in the book value of the asset reported on the Balance Sheet. Comparing two companies who appear to have the same amount of initial asset investment, the company using straight-line depreciation will report lower depreciation, thus higher profits and a higher asset book value in the early years of the asset, solely because they chose a non-accelerated method of depreciation. Understanding the cause and effect of the different depreciation methods should aid the investor in interpreting the accounting results.

Another example to illustrate this point is the inventory cost basis selected by a company. Although cash flow will not be different, reported earnings will be affected. To illustrate, if the firm identifies their inventory cost method as LIFO based, the more recent (and in a period of rising prices) higher dollar value will be recorded as the cost of the sale in the current period, thus reducing reported profits. Simultaneously, the Balance Sheet will report inventory on a comparably undervalued basis since it maintains the older and lower cost basis as the existing inventory layers. In contrast, a company who selects FIFO will report lower cost of sales, therefore higher profits while valuing inventory of current costs. Once again, understanding the impact of the accounting alternative chosen by a company is important in analyzing the reported financial results.

Changes in Business Ownership

Changes in business ownership, i.e., acquisition or disposal of affiliated businesses or discontinuance of a segment of the business, also receive footnote disclosure. Often the acquisitions and disposals are identified in separate notes.

The information contained in this note details major acquisitions and provides data on the acquired business: when it was acquired, the amount paid for acquisition as well as how the purchase price was financed, i.e., cash, debt or equity issue, and how the acquisition was accounted for. Most acquisitions are recorded under the "purchase" accounting method and result in the operations of the company acquired being consolidated into the reported results of the acquiring company from the date of acquisition. In addition, any value paid in excess of the fair market value of the assets acquired, i.e., goodwill, is identified with the resulting amortization period noted.

Note disclosures on divestitures of a company normally detail the company sold, the selling price, the amount of gain or loss recognized on the transaction, and the tax effect of such a transaction. In contrast, discontinued operations are the result of a disposal of a "segment" of business operations. The information presented for discontinued operations is similar to that of the sale of a primary business, i.e., what was sold, the selling price, and the amount of gain or loss recognized in the transaction.

The Investor's View of Acquisitions, Divestitures and Discontinued Operations

The note disclosure on acquisitions, divestitures, and discontinued operations provides an indication of the company's management philosophy and identifies any shift in focus for the company's operations. It also allows an investor to judge management's ability to fulfill its stated goals and to determine whether a business acquisition or disposal is inconsistent with the stated business plan. For example, if a steel company has stated that it will return to its primary steel making business operation but continues to acquire unrelated businesses or does not sell the existing unrelated business, an investor must determine how the apparent inconsistency between stated business objectives and actual business events affects the company's ability to operate. Acquisitions of unrelated businesses may be a sign that the company does not anticipate significant growth opportunities within its current line of business.

Other more specific information is usable by investors from the acquisition and divestiture note disclosures. If the note identified an acquisition, the method of financing the purchase is important to an investor. If the purchase was paid for with cash, does that decision result in a company with limited opportunities because of restricted cash flow? Cash limitations also affect investors since it impacts the company's ability to pay dividends.

If the purchase was accomplished by issuing debt, investors must inquire whether the long-term financing of the purchase restricts the company's opportunity for additional growth and expansion because of a debt level that is too high. An alternative, the issuing of stock to help finance an acquisition, also has implications for an investor since the increased shares tend to dilute the ownership of the company, decrease reported EPS and increase the cash requirements for dividends.

Likewise the divestiture or segment disposal must be evaluated by the investor. Did the company sell the business or segment at a substantial loss? If so, did the desire or need to sell the company justify the loss incurred on the transaction? Another pertinent question is how will the proceeds from the sale or disposal be used? Was the sale transacted for cash or did the company accept a financing arrangement? If a financing arrangement was accepted, what are the terms of such an arrangement and what is the company's recourse in the event of default?

The information contained in the note disclosure will aid an investor in trying to answer these questions, all of which affect the investor's decision-making process.

Note Disclosures on Debt

All annual reports contain a footnote disclosure on the debt of a company, often both short-term debt (due within one year) and long-term debt (due after one year). The type and amount of debt information disclosed is of particular interest to an investor.

The note disclosure on long-term debt normally begins with a detailed schedule of debt. This schedule will identify the type of debt, such as debentures, notes or mortgages or commercial paper, and will usually classify the debt as secured or unsecured. It will further detail the interest rates and maturities of the individual debt instrument or issue. The note disclosure is also required to identify the amount of debt due in each of the next five years and in the aggregate after that period. Thus an investor is clearly able to see the amount due, when it is due, and the interest cost of maintaining the debt security.

As a further aid to investors, the note disclosure will also identify any bond sinking fund or loan covenant requirements. These requirements often contain limitations on dividends or other borrowing and are of prime interest to an investor since they indicate potential restrictions for future growth or opportunities. Additional information on the company's debt arrangements, such as financing agreements, revolving credit agreements, letters and lines of credit, compensating balance requirements, and loan guarantees or commitments are also provided and form a data base for evaluation by an investor.

The Investor's View of Debt Disclosures

An investor's evaluation of a company's debt structure provides an overall assessment of the short-term and long-term commitments of the organization and their impact on the present and future financial position. Of particular concern is the amount of leverage of the organization, the ability of the company to carry such debt, and any limitation the debt imposes on the company's operations and financial position.

An investor is specifically concerned with the impact of the debt on cash flow for both interest and principal requirements of long-term and short-term commitments. Further restrictions on the company due to loan covenants or bond sinking fund requirements indicate a limitation on the company's operations, management, and flexibility to respond to changes in its operating environment. The amount and type of assets pledged against secured debt as well as the type and amount of available credit sources also provide an indication of a company's ability to function effectively.

A final consideration for an investor looking for return on his investment is any restriction on the company's ability to pay dividends. Obviously an investor would want to carefully examine the type of debt outstanding and its restriction or potential restrictions on dividend payout since this would directly affect the potential rate of return.

Note Disclosures on Lease Commitments

A lease is an agreement that allows one party to use an asset for a stated period of time in exchange for a periodic payment. However, the terms of the lease agreement must be examined to determine whether a transfer of ownership interest exists. If the transfer of ownership interest is not present, the lease is classified as an operating lease with annual rent commitments recorded as rental expense in the current period. If a transfer of ownership interest does exist, the lease is classified as a capital lease resulting in a long-term commitment with transfer of asset interest to the lessee. This transfer of interest requires recognition of the asset and corresponding liability by the lessee.

The significant increase in the use of leasing as a financing alternative began in the 1970's and created the need for a separate detailed disclosure in the annual report (although some companies still report lease commitments in the debt note disclosure). Effectively, lease commitments represent much of the same obligation that other debt instruments carry, i.e., the commitment of future resources in exchange for an asset in the current period. Leases are often the financing alternative chosen in the acquisition of plant and equipment.

The note disclosure provides information on both operating and capital leases and classifies the lease obligation as current or long term. The note will also identify the leased assets, the executory costs associated with such assets, e.g., taxes, maintenance and insurance, the expiration date of the lease and the rental expense for the current period.

In a manner similar to the debt disclosure, the lease disclosures will show the minimum rent commitments under non-cancellable operating and capital leases by year for 5 years and in the aggregate after that time period. In addition, the note will show the present value of the non-current capital leases.

The Investor's View of Lease Disclosures

An investor must examine lease commitments in a manner similar to the debt instruments since the impact of the lease commitments is identical to other debt arrangements. Effectively, the lease commitments represent debt and as such require the servicing of the debt with periodic payments which include interest and principal.

It is important for an investor to consider lease commitments when evaluating the present and future financial position of the company. Determining a company's overall ability to carry debt, its future cash flow requirements, other available credit sources, and the restrictions imposed by such debt arrangements are all primary considerations.

Note Disclosures on Pensions

Pension obligations represent a company's commitment to their employees during retirement years based on the services rendered by employees in earlier years. This liability often represents a significant commitment of resources by a company. The note disclosure requirements on pensions are the longest and most complex of any note information. In reality, they are probably the least understood of all the financial transactions; yet, their impact on the company's operations and financial condition is substantial.

The note disclosure describes the funded status and the Balance Sheet provisions for a company's pension plans, both U.S. based plans and plans covering foreign operations. The specific footnote details are usually broken down into two areas. The first provides general information on

- who the plan covers (U.S. or foreign),

- whether it is contributory or non-contributory (i.e., whether the employee pays or the company pays),

- whether it is defined benefit plan or a defined contribution plan (i.e., whether the plan is based on a specific retirement benefit or a currently specified contribution),

- how the benefits are determined (years of service, average earnings etc.),

- a summary of the current year's pension cost (as shown on the current period Statement of Income),

- the funding policy (i.e., how the plan assets are accumulated),

- how plan assets are invested (corporate stocks and bonds, real estate, government securities, etc.) and

- discount rates used.

The second portion of the note disclosure usually describes the funded status of the plan. The specific details identified are the

- actuarial present value of the benefit obligations,

- fair market value of the plan assets,

- net pension liability or asset,

- plan assets in excess of the projected benefit obligation or the benefit obligation in excess of the plan assets,

- unrecognized gain or loss,

- unrecognized prior service cost and

- unrecognized net asset.

It should be obvious from the information shown above, that the financial statement presentation of the pension obligations is complex and that their impact on the financial position of a company are difficult to understand. However, there are certain aspects concerning pensions that an investor should consider when evaluating a company.

The Investor's View of Pensions

Although an investor will often not comprehend all the complexities of pension accounting, there is certain information that the investor should consider. It is important for the investor to realize that pensions represent a significant commitment of future resources but that the amounts are recorded in the present and are based on actuarial estimates and projections. Thus adjustments to the data must always be considered.

Specific information regarding current period reporting of pension data focuses in two key areas. The first is the amount of pension expense recognized in the present year on the Statement of Income. The second and probably the most important is whether the projected benefit obligation (i.e., the liability for future payments) is in excess of the pension plan assets (resources available), and, therefore, the pension plan is underfunded. Unfunded pension liabilities are a form of debt and should be treated as such. In this situation, there should be an accrued liability for pension obligations on the Balance Sheet.

An investor may also observe the inverse of the above situation, i.e., the plan assets are in excess of the projected future benefit obligation. This situation creates an overfunding of the pension plan and a corresponding prepaid pension fund asset would be found on the Balance

Sheet. Firms with substantial overfunded pension plans may become takeover targets as the overfunded pension plan constitutes a potential source of cash.

A further item for an investor to consider is the reasonableness of the assumptions used. For example, the rate of return on the plan assets noted in the footnote disclosure should appear reasonable in light of the current economic conditions. For example, many companies have recently increased their assumed rate of return on plan assets. If their rates of return are not achieved, the pension plan is liable to become underfunded, resulting in a drain on future corporate cash flows. An investor should also consider the reasonableness of the discount rates used in the projections, as well as the projected increases in compensations levels. For example, if a firm with a defined benefit plan underestimates future compensation levels, it will put aside inadequate funds for meeting future obligations.

Although an investor needs to consider the pension obligation of a company, they must also consider a company's liability for future events that are not uniformly recorded and reported in the financial statements, notably, the liability for health-care and life-insurance benefits that are also promised to employees upon retirement. Although there are many similarities between the pension obligation and health care/life insurance obligations, at present, the costs of these obligations are expensed in the year in which they are paid and no liability appears on the Balance Sheet for the future obligation. There is presently a change requiring companies to record and report their expense and obligation in a manner similar to that of pensions but the ruling is not effective until fiscal years beginning after December of 1992. Once again the implementation of this requirement will require recognition of a substantial liability.

Note Disclosures on Income Taxes

This topic is also complex and an investor needs to recognize that the current period expense will be reported on the Statement of Income while the obligation for tax payments is shown in the liability portion of the Balance Sheet. Thus, taxes represent a drain on future resources for the amount of the payments deferred to future periods.

The amount of income reported on the Income Statement is not usually equal to the income used to calculate the tax liability. These differences arise because of the manner in which certain items are reported for accounting purposes versus the method in which they are reported for tax purposes. For example, a company will often choose straight-line depreciation for accounting purposes while choosing an accelerated method, currently MACRS (Modified Accelerated Cost Recovery System), for tax purposes. Thus an asset will be depreciated differently for accounting and tax purposes resulting in different reported income amounts. Correspondingly, different income tax expense (based on accounting income) and income tax liability (based on taxable income) will be reported.

The note disclosure on income taxes usually shows the components of the provision for income tax (the annual expenses) for federal, state, local and foreign taxes. It will also show the current and deferred portions of the provision, the amounts paid, and a reconciliation of the effective tax rate with the stated federal tax rate. With the implementation of FASB Standard #96 in 1992, the calculations for determining deferred taxes must be done under the liability method. This will alter the footnote disclosure accordingly.

The investor's view of income taxes is fairly limited, i.e., the amount of the tax liability reported on the Balance Sheet represents a drain on future resources. However, there is little additional evaluation necessary.

Note Disclosures on Segment and Quarterly Reporting

Segment reporting is specifically required by accounting regulation and provides information on the different operating segments within a company. A segment is usually defined as any operation which generates more than 10% of the total revenues, total profits/losses or total assets of all operating segments combined. On occasion, the information is also shown by geographic region, foreign operations, and major customers.

The investor is often aided by segment reporting. The information allows an investor to see the small pieces of the much bigger puzzle thereby highlighting key information useful in the investment decision-making process. Such information can help when forecasting future income and expenses.

Note information on quarterly reporting usually appears as one of the last footnotes and contains key operating information, such as operating revenues, operating expenses, income/loss from continuing operations and EPS (earnings per share). The time frame shown usually is at least 8 quarters (2 years) and often a three year (12 quarter) period is shown. The sum of the quarterly data for the year will equal the amounts reported in the annual report with one exception, EPS. Since EPS is calculated based on a weighted average number of shares of stock outstanding, the individual quarterly calculation will provide different results when recalculated on an annualized basis.

The investor should use quarterly data as an additional data source. This type of information allows the investor to see trends or seasonality within the reporting year. However, it is important to remember that the quarterly data is unaudited data, and, as such, the annual report data is more reliable.

Note Disclosures on Contingencies

Contingencies, also shown as contingent liabilities, are potential liabilities incurred by a company. These contingencies impact present events but the amounts cannot be reliably estimated at the present time. Examples of contingencies are pending lawsuits, purchase guarantees or commitments, pending sales or acquisitions etc.

When faced with a potential liability, companies must determine whether the outcome of the event and the corresponding expense or revenue are probable, reasonably possible or remote. If the event is probable and the amount can be reasonably estimated, the amount of the contingency will be recorded in the accounting records if it is an expense or a loss. If the probable amount is a gain, or the events are only reasonably possible or remote, the event will be described only in the footnote disclosure.

Investors should closely examine the information contained in this footnote. If an investor wants a sense of events which have not yet impacted the financial condition of the company, but may substantially impact the future financial condition of the company, the information can be found in this footnote.

Stock Options/Stock Compensation Plans

This footnote describes the stock option plans available within the company. These plans are often used as compensation or incentive plans for employees. The note disclosure will detail the terms of the plan, such as the amount of options issued, the option price, the dates of grant, and exercise and expiration. In addition, the number of the options granted, exercised, and cancelled are shown as well as the number of stock options still outstanding.

An investor should assess the information on the stock option plans in terms of their ownership position. If the exercise of options takes place, the company will receive cash proceeds, thereby increasing cash flow. However, the increased number of shares issued will dilute the investors relative ownership position. In addition, the reported earnings per share amount will be reduced whether or not the stock options are exercised as long as they are potentially exercisable (in accordance with the requirements of EPS calculations).

Other Footnote Disclosures

The above discussion did not intend to exhaust the list of footnote disclosures, rather it was to emphasize the more significant notes. However, there are a wide variety of other footnote disclosures often shown in the annual report. Among those most common are notes detailing the following:

- the changes in equity (assuming that there was not a separate financial statement showing this information),

- earnings per share calculations,

- credit arrangements (e.g., lines of credit available),

- plant and equipment,

- intangibles,

- research and development,

- foreign currency activity and translations, and

- short-term liabilities.

Each of these footnote disclosures aids the investor in understanding, evaluating and analyzing a company's financial position, and the results of operations.

As a further aid to investors, financial statement analysis should be performed.

CHAPTER 7

FINANCIAL STATEMENT ANALYSIS

Although financial statements contain the wealth of information detailed in the previous chapters, it is the analysis of that information that allows an investor to correctly interpret the financial status of a company.

Financial statements serve a multitude of purposes for both the company that produces them and for investors. However, they are not always looked upon in a positive light. In the October 4, 1988, East Coast Edition of *The Wall Street Journal,* Henry F. Hill summarized the pitfalls of financial statements in a poem entitled "Reading Matters":

> Before you invest
> Always read the prospectus.
> It's required by laws
> Designed to protect us.
> Buried somewhere therein
> Under mountains of prose
> Are all the risks
> To which you're exposed.
> Don't know where to start?
> Let me give you a hint:
> The greater the hazard,
> The smaller the print.

Although this indicates a somewhat skeptical perspective of financial statements, it introduces a common and necessary viewpoint: an investor must always read financial statements with a critical, if not skeptical, point of view.

The discussion in Chapters 1-6 focused on the financial statements. This was necessary in order to obtain the background and perspective needed to proceed with financial statement analysis as a separate and distinct discipline. This analysis is highlighted in the following pages.

What Is Financial Statement Analysis?

Financial statement analysis is a logical and systematic method of examining and summarizing financial statement data. It is usually accomplished by organizing financial data into a succinct and manageable
information base designed to answer specific questions for the investor.
The questions that it will answer depend upon the perspective and
information needs of the investor.

The information presented in this book was designed to provide
an investor with an understanding of a company's operating results and
financial position as indicated by the published financial statement data.
This chapter will introduce tools and techniques that can be used to
further aid in the analysis of a company's financial statements. As the
discussion moves to financial statement analysis, it is important to reit-
erate that one cannot obtain an adequate understanding nor perform a
meaningful analysis of financial statements for a single year. Analysis
of the numbers themselves can be performed but without a basis for
comparison, the value of such an analysis is questionable.

Why Should an Investor Perform
Financial Statement Analysis?

A primary reason investors should perform financial statement analysis
is to summarize, highlight and integrate key financial information. Strategic pieces of financial data are often shown in different sections of the
financial statements. For instance, working capital availability is not
shown as a line-item in the financial statements, yet it is often considered
by investors to be a key piece of financial information. Instead, information on net working capital must be calculated by subtracting total
current liabilities from total current assets. And, as we will see, further
analysis of such information is necessary before deciding whether the
amount of available working capital is adequate given the needs of the
company.

Financial statement analysis is also used to establish benchmark
information for comparison purposes. Any piece of financial information
is valuable only if it can be compared to a similar measure from a
different time period or for another company or economic aggregate. In
addition, risk assessment is particularly important for an investor and
performing financial statement analysis aids in this assessment. With the
assimilation of information, it is easier to assign priorities to the apparent
risk factors.

Financial statement analysis is also performed to ascertain the
overall financial health of a firm. Identification of a company's financial

strengths and weaknesses is a prerequisite for any investment decision. The debt and equity structure, cash flow activity, debt level, and asset management are a few of the critical questions that must be answered in the analysis process.

Trend analysis is important when performing financial statement analysis. Investors study the past in the hopes of gaining insight into the future, and trend analysis helps to develop this insight. An investor might ask "how many years of financial data constitute a 'trend'?" Although there is no specific rule, it is commonly accepted that the minimum should be at least five years and eight to ten years is preferable. An analysis should always try to encompass a business cycle so as to observe the sensitivity of the business to a recession. If an investor examines published annual reports, trend analysis data is often presented for 10 or 15 years. This enables an investor to perform an in-depth, long-term analysis of the financial results.

The Benefits and Limitations of Financial Statement Analysis

Although an investor should perform financial statement analysis before making an investment decision, it is important that the benefits as well as the limitations of such an analysis are thoroughly understood.

One of the primary benefits of financial statement analysis is its ability to provide a summary of financial statement information. With such a summarization, the financial statement data becomes more manageable, thereby facilitating the decision making process. An additional benefit of the summarized information is that it becomes easier for an investor to identify the strengths and weaknesses of a company.

The limitations of such a process must also be considered. Although financial statement analysis provides a summary of the information, such a summary may in fact cause an investor to lose sight of the larger issues. The financial statement analysis process may also provide information on the financial elements without respect to how the elements are related; although, the summary information may make the data more manageable, it does not prioritize the information for analysis purposes.

Although such a process allows for easier identification of the company's strengths and weaknesses, it does not tell an investor how to capitalize on the strengths nor how to eliminate the weaknesses. In addition, the analysis process does not answer the questions that such a process raises. For example, although the summary process might identify a company with a debt level that is considered excessive, the analysis will not necessarily suggest a means of reducing the debt to a manageable level.

In summary, it is important for an investor to remember three things when discussing financial statement analysis. First, financial statement analysis is meaningless without comparative data, i.e., at least several years financial information for the company under consideration and relevant industry statistics. Second, financial statement analysis uses historical data which is not necessarily indicative of future performance. Third, and perhaps most importantly, financial statement analysis does not replace an investor's need to make decisions, it simply acts as an aid in such a process. If investors consider the strengths as well as the weaknesses of the financial statement analysis, they will be well served in the decision making process.

What Data Is Needed To Perform Financial Statement Analysis?

An investor needs a complete data base in order to make an informed decision. Included in this data base is specific information on the company under consideration, for example, financial statements for a three year period. That does not necessarily mean three annual reports since companies are required to present at least two years data for comparative purposes in each annual report and many companies actually provide three years information in each annual report.

This information is then used by an investor in trend analysis. The primary advantage of trend analysis is its ability to put the current year's financial results into perspective. Current year financial data has limited value unless it can be compared to the equivalent of a "base" year or years. With such a comparison, fluctuations and reporting consistencies or inconsistencies, are identifiable.

A complete data base should also include common-size statements for the same time period discussed above, i.e., at least three years. Common-size statements reduce each financial statement element to a common denominator, for example, a common-size Statement of Income will show each of the statement items as a percentage of sales. Assuming sales as 100%, cost of goods sold might be shown as 54% and sales salary expense might be shown as 21%. Although common-size statements are not typically part of the published financial reporting package, they are easy to calculate and facilitate the comparison between reporting periods and between companies of different size.

A further requirement for a financial statement analysis data base is industry specific information, which can be obtained from publications such as Prentice Hall's *The Almanac of Business and Financial Ratios,* and Dun & Bradstreet Credit Service's *Industry Norms and Financial Ratios.* The use of industry standard information has several benefits. First, its use gives an objective standard by which a given company's results can be measured. This use of a yardstick measurement is important and is similar to using several years results as a base measure when comparing intra-company financial information.

Another advantage of industry standard information is that it represents the "norm" or average of a large number of companies. As a result, wide fluctuations by any one company are blended in the average, and the risk of comparing companies who have unusual circumstances is reduced. More importantly, proper use of this information allows one to compare results between companies who are in the same industry and who face many of the same problems.

Although the use of industry standard information has many advantages, there are some distinct disadvantages which must be considered. Since industry information is normally reported by industry classification, it is important for a company to properly identify their primary industry group. At present this is a major problem because of the large corporate conglomerates often result from mergers and acquisitions. For instance, American Brands 1987 annual report indicates that they operate in five different industry segments: tobacco, financial services, distilled spirits, office products, and consumer products. Because the majority of their reported financial data is presented as total company results, it is difficult to identify and incorporate meaningful standard financial information for comparison purposes.

A second problem that exists with the use of standard industry information is the timeliness of the reporting. For example, in the 1990 edition of the *Almanac of Business and Industrial Financial Ratios,* the actual data compiled was for the time period between July 1986 and June 1987. Because of such a time lag, it is difficult to obtain up-to-date financial results unless an investor has access to a computerized data base which provides current data.

A further consideration is the size of the companies that comprise the industry statistics. To illustrate, assume that a company is a small computer manufacturer and uses the statistics for the entire computer industry for comparison purposes. Obviously, the relevancy of the comparison is substantially diminished since their operating, management and accounting problems are probably very different from the many large companies in this industry classification. Even if this company were to use financial information that was further broken down by size of company, there may not be enough smaller companies in the particular industry to reflect true average results.

A final, yet substantial, issue to consider is the tendency to assume that if specific company results are different from the industry standard, that the particular company must have a problem or, conversely, must be doing better than average. For example, if the industry standard for return on owners equity is 15% and Company A's return is 25%, it is easy to think that the company has performed well above the average. Upon further investigation, it may be determined that the primary increase in the return was caused by a large repurchase of the company's stock. As a result, the perceived improvement was simply a matter of a reduced number of shares outstanding, not improved operating results.

Although the use of industry standard information can be helpful and is often necessary in the financial analysis process, it is imperative for an investor to remember the constraints involved in their usage.

How Does an Investor Perform Financial Statement Analysis?

An investor typically begins financial statement analysis by thoroughly reading the financial statements, particularly common size statements, and identifying trends in the reported information. This process is substantially aided by the performance of ratio analysis. Since ratio analysis is a significant component of financial statement analysis, the remainder of this chapter will be devoted to this topic.

Ratio Analysis

There are a wide variety of financial ratios presented in finance, accounting, and management books typically broken down into liquidity ratios, profitability ratios, operating or activity ratios, and capital structure ratios (often referred to as leverage ratios). However, the presentation of these ratios as distinct topics often clouds the analysis. It is not necessarily a specific ratio that is important; rather, it is the interrelationship between certain key ratios that will provide the information needed by investors.

As a result, this chapter will focus on the significant financial management issues faced by a business, specifically liquidity or the adequacy of working capital, profitability and long-term solvency. The discussion will further identify the relevant ratios that can be used by investors to evaluate a company's financial position from each of these perspectives.

Liquidity

Liquidity is defined as the ability of a company to pay short-term debt obligations as they come due. As a result, cash flow is a significant consideration. Because the Statement of Cash Flows (as described in Chapter 4) is a historically based financial statement, it often is of limited use to an investor trying to project future cash flows. Thus investors will often use liquidity ratios (such as the current and quick ratio) and operating activity ratios (such as receivable and inventory turnover ratios) as indications of cash flow activity. It is important to remember that a complete cash flow analysis is critical in the decision making process and that the discussion of liquidity in this chapter must not be considered a replacement for cash flow analysis.

Liquidity assessment requires information on the current asset and current liability balances. Liquidity is also affected by the management of short-term operating assets, most notably, accounts receivable and inventory. If an investor wants to assess a company's liquidity position, the following ratios should be examined:

Ratio	Calculation
Current ratio	$\dfrac{\text{current assets}}{\text{current Liabilities}}$
Quick ratio or Acid test ratio	$\dfrac{\text{cash + marketable securities + receivables}}{\text{current liabilities}}$
Accounts Receivable: Turnover	$\dfrac{\text{credit sales for the period}}{\text{accounts receivable}}$
Collection period	$\dfrac{\text{number of days in the period}}{\text{accounts receivable turnover}}$
Inventory: Turnover	$\dfrac{\text{cost of goods sold}}{\text{inventory}}$
Days Sales outstanding in payables	$\dfrac{\text{number of days in the period}}{\text{accounts payable turnover}}$
Accounts payable Turnover	$\dfrac{\text{purchases for the period}}{\text{accounts payable}}$
Days Purchases outstanding in payables	$\dfrac{\text{number of days in the period}}{\text{accounts payable turnover}}$

The current ratio, current assets divided by current liabilities, is used by almost every user of financial information. It is a measurement device that provides a quick and easy assessment of the company's short-term financial position, i.e., a company's ability to meet its short-term debt obligations. It can also be used to measure a firm's ability to effectively manage its short-term assets and corresponding short-term liabilities.

The primary advantage of the current ratio is the ease of calculation since properly formatted financial statements clearly indicate total current asset and liability information. The primary disadvantage is that it doesn't consider the individual elements comprising current assets. The ratio assumes that all current assets have equal value and possess the same ability to reduce short-term debt obligations.

As the following example illustrates, the quality of the current asset elements can be substantially different. To demonstrate, examine the financial information found below in Figure 7-1.

In this example, it appears that both companies have the same liquidity position, i.e., they have $1.33 in asset dollars that can be used to pay off one dollar of short-term debt. However, if the individual elements comprising total current assets are examined, differences in their liquidity position become apparent.

Recalling that liquidity is the ability to use current assets to pay off current liabilities on a dollar for dollar basis, Company B is actually in a more liquid position. At the present time, their cash and marketable securities total 56% of their short-term assets. In addition, further conversion of these assets is not necessary since they are effectively in cash form. However, Company A has only 25% of their assets in a cash or near cash position. Any additional or unanticipated cash requirements

---

Figure 7-1   Financial Statement Data

Account	Company A	Company B
Cash	$100,000	$100,000
Marketable Securities	100,000	350,000
Accounts Receivable	300,000	200,000
Inventory	250,000	100,000
Prepaids	50,000	50,000
Total Current Assets	$800,000	$800,000
Total Current Liabilities	$600,000	$600,000
Current Ratio	1.33:1	1.33:1

---

would dictate that the accounts receivable and/or inventory be converted to cash before the normal operating cycle was completed, most likely resulting in cash flow substantially below the face value of the asset. For example, a company experiencing a cash flow shortage is unlikely to be able to sell inventory to raise cash especially if the inability to sell additional products is a cause of the initial liquidity crisis. To gain additional insight, an investor is able to obtain better liquidity information that considers the differences in asset cash value by examining the quick or acid-test ratio.

Quick or Acid-Test Ratio

The quick ratio, expressed as cash plus marketable securities and receivables divided by current liabilities, overcomes some of the disadvantages associated with the current ratio. Because this ratio is designed to measure the firm's ability to pay off current debts quickly, it introduces a time parameter. Using the sample data found in Figure 7-1, the quick ratios can be calculated as .83:1 (500,000 ÷ 600,000) for Company A and 1.08:1 (650,000 ÷ 600,000) for Company B. It is now easy to see that Company B is more liquid, consistent with our analysis in the discussion on the limitations of the current ratio.

Unfortunately, there is still a limitation to the use of the quick ratio since it considers accounts receivable to have cash value equal to its face amount. As the discussion in the current ratio section indicated, this is not usually the case. Conversion of accounts receivable into cash (by selling, factoring, assigning or otherwise pledging accounts receivable to a bank or other financial institution), particularly·under forced circumstances, will not yield cash equal to the face amount of.the current receivable balance.

As the discussion indicates, an investor cannot examine the current and quick ratios as a sole indicator of liquidity because of the differences in asset composition. Further consideration must be given to the management of the asset accounts affected by current operations, specifically inventory and accounts receivable.

Accounts Receivable Ratios

Accounts receivable turnover and collection period ratios defined earlier indicate the ability of the firm to convert their credit based sales into cash receipts. For example, the turnover ratio examines credit sales for the period in relation to the outstanding accounts receivable balance. Therefore, if the credit sales for the period were $200,000 and the outstanding accounts receivable balance is $50,000, the accounts receivable were converted to cash on average four times during the period.

However, this information is not as beneficial as knowing the number of days it takes to collect on the receivables, thus, the average collection period is very important. If the time period involved in the previous example is a quarter or 90 days, the average collection period would be 22 1/2 days (90 days/turnover of 4).

The information obtained has to relate to an operating statistic to be meaningful. The most relevant statistic is the credit terms under which the sales occurred. If the invoice specified payments terms of 30 days, an average collection period of 22 1/2 days is excellent, if the credit terms were 10 days, there is a problem with timely collection of accounts receivable.

Another consideration is the sales trend for the current period. If sales increased for the period, and the average collection period increased, there is a higher base of financial assets which are not being managed properly. In addition, a higher sales volume and higher average collection period might also indicate that the firm is granting credit to riskier accounts. This policy might in turn increase bad debt expense. Increased sales are not beneficial unless they can be turned into increased cash receipts.

What does this information mean to the investor? Primarily, these ratios indicate how well a company is managing a critical component of cash flow, i.e., the ability to convert credit sales to cash needed for operations.

Inventory Ratios

Often thought to be the most critical operating area, proper inventory management is essential to a financially healthy company. Inventory ratios measure how often the company is able to turn over their inventory. For example, the inventory turnover examines the cost of goods sold in relation to the inventory balance. If the resulting turnover rate is low, it may be an indication of excess inventory levels, or possibly obsolete inventory.

Examining the inventory turnover for a company, assume that a company has annual cost of goods sold of $1,000,000 and the inventory balance is $200,000. This information shows that the company can only turn over their inventory five times a year. This turnover rate may be acceptable for a company who produces non-perishable goods, but it is hardly reasonable for a produce or dairy manufacturer.

It is also important to examine the days sales outstanding in inventory. If the company's inventory turnover rate is only five times a year, it means that they are maintaining 73 days inventory (365 - 5 turnover rate) at any point in time. Again, the relevant question is whether 73 days represents excess commitment to inventory levels. Of course, there are disadvantages to substantially reducing the inventory levels, such as lost sales due to "stockout," but they are usually balanced by the benefits of a more efficient inventory management system. Excess commitment to inventory is a drain on the available working capital of a company. Unfortunately, investors often fail to recognize that funds tied up in inventory, a non-income-earning asset, could be invested elsewhere to increase the profitability of the firm.

Accounts Payable Ratios

Although the focus on liquidity is often asset oriented, the management of the accounts payable function is also a determinant of a company's ability to remain liquid. Proper management of the payables function dictates that invoices be paid in a manner which focuses on cash outflows at the latest possible time, balancing the value of early payment discounts against the cash flow needs of the company. Thus the accounts payable activity ratios must also be examined in conjunction with the current, quick receivables and inventory ratios.

Accounts payable ratios represent the opposite of the accounts receivable ratios, indicating how often the company pays off their accounts payable balance and how long the payables remain outstanding. Thus the accounts payable turnover, which examines the purchases for the period in relation to the accounts payable balance, as well as the days purchases outstanding in payables (the relevant time period divided by the turnover), must be examined.

As an illustration, assume that a company has credit purchases for the quarterly period of $100,000, and that the present accounts payable balance is $40,000. Calculation of accounts payable turnover for the quarter yields a rate of 2 1/2 times. Again, the more meaningful information is obtained from the days outstanding in accounts payable. Calculation of this number shows that the company payables are outstanding for a period of 36 days (90 days in the quarter divided by 2 1/2).

Consideration must be given to the invoice payments terms from the suppliers. If the invoice specifies terms of 60 days, the company is not optimally managing their accounts payable function since they paid earlier than needed. Conversely, if the payment terms are 30 days, and late fees are assessed, the additional cost of delaying payment outweighs the benefit of preserving the cash flow.

This ratio must also be examined in relation to the levels of inventory purchases. Increased purchases of inventory needed to support increased sales activity will usually cause an increase in accounts payable levels. However, an increase in accounts payable might also indicate a cash flow problem. Improper management of the payable function can have negative impact on the daily operating activities and possibly affect the company's ability to buy on credit in the future.

Working Capital

An additional, often-cited financial statistic in the discussion of liquidity is working capital. Net working capital, defined as current assets minus current liabilities, indicates the dollars available for use on items other than current debt requirements and indicates the ability of a company to support growth. While working capital measured in dollars is often reviewed by analysts, it does not add to the analysis of working capital adequacy. It is the relationship between current assets and current liabilities that is important, not the total amount of working capital, as shown by the data on the two companies below:

	Firm A	Firm B
Current Assets	$300,000	$4,000,000
Current Liabilities	100,000	3,000,000
New Working Capital	$200,000	$1,000,000

While Firm B has five times as much working capital as Firm A, it is obviously much less liquid.

A further illustration of the deficiency of expressing working capital ratio on a raw dollar basis rather than in relative terms, is illustrated as follows. Suppose Company C has current assets of $1,200,000 and current liabilities of $600,000. Further, assume that Company D has current assets of $2,000,000 and current liabilities of $1,400,000. Calculation of working capital as current assets minus current liabilities indicates that both companies have equal working capital of $600,000. Although it appears that both firms have equal financial position, the current ratio shows a 2:1 ratio for Company C and a 1.4:1 for Company D.

Although there are shortcomings in analyzing working capital from an investor's perspective, one area in which it is helpful is to consider working capital as a percentage of sales. Such an examination indicates the incremental working capital needs caused by additional sales dollars. This measurement can be very helpful as a planning device since it measures the efficient use of available or needed resources.

The above discussion of liquidity analysis emphasizes a significant point concerning the use of financial ratios, i.e., no single ratio should ever be used as an indication of a firm's financial position. Only when the results of related ratios are examined and interpreted in tandem can an investor accurately assess the financial results. Thus, from a liquidity perspective, the current and quick ratios must be examined in conjunction with the activity ratios for receivables, inventory, and payables.

Profitability

Profitability is the second area requiring analysis for an investor. Profit is generated when a company earns revenue in excess of expenses incurred, and is reflected as net income on The Statement of Income. To assess the type, quality, efficiency and value of the reported earnings, an investor should examine profitability ratios. If an investor considers profitability ratios as an overall assessment of The Statement of Income, these ratios can be extremely flexible, open-ended, creative and informative.

It is important that an investor develop an understanding of the basic factors underlying profitability in order to assess future prospects of an investment. To facilitate such an understanding, an investor should study the primary components of profitability and their interrelationships—namely, earnings per share (EPS), return on equity (ROE), and return on assets (ROA).

The definition of, and interrelationship between, these primary elements of profitability can be shown as noted below (other often used profitability ratios will be discussed later in this chapter):

$$\text{Earnings per share (EPS)} = \frac{\text{Earnings Available to Common Stockholders (EAC)}}{\text{Average Number of Shares of Common Stock Outstanding (Average Shares)}}$$

$$\text{EPS} = \frac{\text{EAC}}{\text{Average Shares}} = \frac{\text{EAC}}{\text{Owners Equity (OE)}} \times \frac{\text{OE}}{\text{Average Shares}}$$

$$\text{Return on Owners Equity} = \frac{\text{EAC}}{\text{OE}} = \frac{\text{EAC}}{\text{Total Assets (TA)}} \times \frac{\text{TA}}{\text{OE}}$$

$$\text{Return on Total Assets} = \frac{\text{EAC}}{\text{TA}} = \frac{\text{EAC}}{\text{Net Sales}} \times \frac{\text{Net Sales}}{\text{TA}}$$

Earnings per Share

Earnings per share measures the income available to common stockholders on a per share basis. The number of shares used in the calculation of this ratio is a weighted average number of shares of common stock outstanding during the time period. This ratio is designed to show how much an individual share of common stock "earned" during a given period. This ratio is used in conjunction with market price of the stock to calculate the price/earnings ratio. In addition, disclosure of earnings per share information is required by both generally accepted accounting principles and the SEC and must be shown on the face of The Statement of Income.

The actual calculation of earnings per share depends upon whether the company has a simple or complex capital structure. A simple capital structure assumes that a company has not issued securities that are potentially dilutive, i.e., convertible into additional shares of common stock. For example, examination of the Balance Sheet in Appendix 1 indicates only one equity stock issued (common stock) and no convertible debt outstanding. Thus the EPS reported on the Statement of Income in the Appendix is a simple EPS calculation. A simple EPS calculation divides the income available to common stockholders (net income less any preferred stock dividends declared or any preferred stock dividends that are cumulative but have not been declared) by a weighted average number of common stock shares outstanding.

A complex structure exists whenever a company issues dilutive or potentially dilutive securities. For example, convertible preferred stock or convertible bonds, stock options or warrants, and stock purchase plans are examples of dilutive or potentially dilutive securities. With a complex capital structure, the EPS calculation becomes extremely complicated requiring a multitude of adjustments to both the numerator and the denominator. If the company has many potentially dilutive securities, which may have a high probability of being converted to common stock, an investor should consider the full diluted earnings per share as the more meaningful EPS amount.

An investor needs to be aware that the EPS information, although simple in its Statement of Income presentation, is the result of a very complex process. An investor should also be aware that EPS can change for two primary reasons: changes in income and/or changes in the number of shares of stock outstanding. Thus an increase in EPS isn't necessarily the result of an increase in earnings. To illustrate, assume in year 1 a company has earnings after preferred stock dividend requirements of $100,000 and 50,000 weighted average shares of stock outstanding with a resulting EPS of $2 per share. Assume that in year 2 earnings increase to $120,000 and the reported EPS increases to $3. Although some of the reported EPS increase is attributable to the increase in earnings, further examination might show that the weighted average shares of stock outstanding were reduced to 40,000 shares because the company reacquired 10,000 shares of its own stock.

An investor must consider the reasons for a company to repurchase its own stock. Companies may do so because they believe the stock is undervalued by the market and it represents a good investment at the current price. In contrast, a company repurchasing its own shares may be a sign that it does not have profitable opportunities within its current line of business. Thus investors must ascertain the reason(s) for any changes in the reported EPS amount rather than assume that any increase in EPS is due to increased earnings.

Return on Equity

Return on equity (ROE), expressed as income available to common stockholders divided by stockholders equity, is the most widely recognized ratio and is accepted as a standard measurement device. It is easy to calculate and important in assessing the overall return to an individual stockholder.

The primary disadvantage of this ratio is its ability to be affected by activities not related to the production of earnings. For example, a company can automatically increase their return on equity from one year to the next, even with identical reported profits, if there is a stock repurchase made by the company during the year. Another way to potentially increase the return on equity is to shift the debt and equity mix of the company to a heavier debt load.

Assume Company A reported $500,000 profit in year 1 and has a present stockholders equity value of $5,000,000. The return on equity is 10%. Assume that in year 2, when reported profits were also $500,000, a stock repurchase program reduced the outstanding shares and corresponding equity value to $4,000,000. As a result, the return on equity for year 2 is 12.5%. The company was no more or less profitable from year 1 to year 2; however, the reduction in stockholders equity was beneficial in terms of return on equity. To complete the analysis, the investor should also examine the specific elements of profitability which can be performed by using the DuPont system of analysis. This method is a perfect application of the principle emphasized heavily in this chapter —financial ratios must be examined and analyzed in tandem. The Du-Pont system does this very effectively by breaking down the elements of return on equity into three primary components. The three components are profitability of the operations, degree of asset utilization, and financial leverage.

For example, using the financial statements in Appendix 1, an investor can calculate a return on owners equity of (-54.4%) for 1989 (net loss of $(185,419) divided by shareholders equity of $340,615) and 6% for 1988 (net income of $31,786 divided by shareholder equity of $525,204). Further analyses of the information using the DuPont system indicates the results illustrated in Figure 7–2.

It is now easy to see the elements that comprise the total return on equity, and each of these changes must be carefully considered by an investor. The overall decrease in return on equity is partially attributable to a significant decline in profitability of operations, partially due to a decline in asset turnover, and is also affected by the increase in the leverage component.

Although ROE is one of the most widely accepted measurements of return performance, for shareholders it has serious potential deficiencies, because it is calculated based on the equity figure listed on the balance sheet (book value). A return on equity of 20% may appear at first glance to indicate a company with superior investment potential. However, unless the investor can purchase the stock at book value, which is unlikely, the ROE figure may significantly overstate the return to an investor considering the purchase of the stock. The investor who buys the stock at four times its current book value per share is really only receiving a return of 5% (20%/4) on his equity purchase. Looking at the current price of the stock relative to the book value per share allows an individual investor to view the return in equity figures more clearly.

Return on Assets

The return on assets ratio, defined as income available to common stockholders divided by total assets, shows how effectively and efficiently a company is using their asset base to generate earnings. Inefficient use of a company's assets represents lost earning power for the organization. The results should be examined in conjunction with the asset turnover ratio discussed later in this chapter.

Other Profitability Ratios

The earlier discussion on profitability focused on the prime elements an investor should quickly identify and analyze—namely, earnings per share, return on equity and return on assets. There are also some additional profitability ratios an investor should consider. These ratios, shown

Figure 7-2

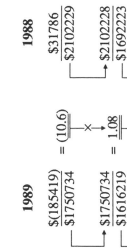

	1989	1988
(1) Profitability of Operations $\left(\frac{NI}{NS}\right)$ – Net Income/Net Sales	$\dfrac{\$(185419)}{\$1750734} = (10.6)$	$\dfrac{\$31786}{\$2102229} = 1.5$
(2) Asset Turnover $\left(\frac{NS}{TA}\right)$ – Net Sales/Total Assets	$\dfrac{\$17750734}{\$1616219} = 1.08$	$\dfrac{\$2102228}{\$1692223} = 1.24$
(3) Leverage $\left(\frac{TA}{OE}\right)$ – Total Assets/Shareholder Equity	$\dfrac{\$1616219}{\$340615} = 4.75$	$\dfrac{\$1692223}{\$525204} = 3.22$
TOTAL RETURN ON EQUITY (Rounded) $\left(\frac{NI}{OE}\right)$ – Net Income (Loss)/Shareholder Equity	$\dfrac{\$(185419)}{\$350615} = (54.4)$	$\dfrac{\$31786}{\$525204} = 6$

or $\dfrac{NI}{SE} \times \dfrac{NS}{TA} \times \dfrac{TA}{OE} = \dfrac{NI}{OE}$

below, emphasize the specific operating elements reported on the Statement of Income.

Ratio	Calculation
Gross profit percentage	$\dfrac{\text{gross profit}}{\text{net sales}}$
Cost of goods sold percentage	$\dfrac{\text{cost of goods sold}}{\text{net sales}}$
Operating expense percentage	$\dfrac{\text{total operating expenses}}{\text{net sales}}$
Income from operations percentage	$\dfrac{\text{income from operations}}{\text{net sales}}$
Net income percentage	$\dfrac{\text{net income}}{\text{net sales}}$
Asset turnover	$\dfrac{\text{net sales}}{\text{net assets}}$

These ratios, when examined in conjunction with earnings per
share, return on equity and return on assets, provide an investor with a
complete picture of a company's reported profitability. Each of these
ratios relate a specific Statement of Income "line item" to net sales. Thus
they effectively restate the Statement of Income results on a common
base.

Discussion of these ratios is often facilitated if the related ratios
are grouped together. For example, one cannot discuss the gross profit
percentage without simultaneously discussing the cost of goods sold
percentage.

Gross Profit and Cost of Goods Sold Percentage

Gross profit represents the sales dollars contribution to other operating
expenses after accounting for the direct cost of the sale, which are
recorded as cost of goods sold. Thus the relationship between gross profit
and cost of goods sold should be obvious, i.e., the combination of the
two must equal total sales. Restating each of these elements on a total
sale basis allows an investor to easily see the relationship between the
related items.

The following example illustrates the point.

	Year 1		Year 2	
	$	%	$	%
Sales	$600,000	100%	$750,000	100%
Cost of Goods Sold	500,000	83.3%	750,000	86.6%
Gross Profit	$100,000	16.7%	$100,000	13.3%

Since sales is 100%, if the gross profit is known, one effectively knows the cost of goods sold and vice versa.

Several observations can be made with respect to the example cited above. Examining the reported information on a dollar basis, the company's gross profit appears to have remained at $100,000. However, if one calculates the gross profit percentage, year 1 was 16.7% and in year 2 it declined to 13.3% while the costs of goods sold rose accordingly from 83.3% to 86.6%.

With the relative change in gross profit, the two elements that comprise gross profit, i.e., product pricing (as reflected in sales) and the cost of production (cost of goods sold) must be evaluated to determine what caused the change and the resulting implications of that change in future events.

Although it is easy to use the gross profit and cost of goods sold percentages to identify changes in cost of goods sold and gross profit, an investor must then relate these changes to the changes in sale and production activity and pricing for the period. Some key questions that should be asked are as follows:

(1)   is the sales increase attributable to an increase in volume, a shift in the product mix sold, or an increase in selling price?

(2)   was the cost of goods sold increase caused by increasing costs of production more than the relative increase in sales?

(3)   how are the changes in gross profit a combination of the changes in #1 and #2?

Using our previous example, sales increased from $600,000 to $750,000, an increase of 25%, while the costs incurred in producing those sales increased 30%. It would appear that the decline in gross margin percentage (from 16.7% to 13.3%) was caused by a production cost increase in excess of the sales increase. To determine the cause of the changes, an investor needs to examine the annual report information provided by company management to answer the three questions posed above.

While the advantage of the gross profit and cost of goods sold ratios are their ability to reduce critical pricing and cost information to a number whose results can be quickly evaluated, there are limits to its usefulness. For example, an investor must use this ratio in conjunction with industry statistics that put the result into perspective. If a company's gross profit percentage was 34% in year 1 and 38% in year 2, it would appear that changes in the company's pricing and/or cost structure had positive results. However, if the industry statistics indicate that the competition maintains a 42% gross profit, the company's results and its importance are altered significantly.

Operating Expense Percentage

The operating expense percentage (total operating expense divided by net sales) indicates a company's ability to control a critical cost category while evaluating increased operating expense in relation to increased sales.

The primary benefit of this ratio is the ease of calculation but only if the financial statement data is structured to show the total operating costs as a single component. At a minimum however, the operating expenses would simply have to be totaled to generate the required total operating costs.

The disadvantage of the ratio is its inability to deal with the specific operating cost components. For instance, general and administrative cost categories contain a wide range of expenses presented in total on The Statement of Income. To use this ratio as an aid in identifying a potential problem area, a more detailed breakdown of costs is required.

Income from Operations Percentage

A critical piece of information, "income from operations," indicates a firm's ability to generate income from their primary operations. In judging the overall long-range ability of a company to continue in existence, an investor must focus on income from operations. Without revenue generated from the primary line of business, a company's status as an ongoing entity becomes questionable.

Income from operations, expressed as a percentage of sales, measures a company's ability to generate profits from the sales of the main product line. Since income from operations is sales minus cost of goods sold and operating costs, it indicates the net operating profit generated per sales dollar. To illustrate, assume sales increased $100,000 from year 1 to year 2, but income from operations as a percentage of sales actually decreased. This would indicate that the operating profit margins were not maintained as sales increased.

The above example provides a good illustration of examining ratios in relation to each other. With a sales increase, but a net profit from operations decrease, further evaluation of the gross profit, cost of goods sold and operating expense data would be necessary. However, because such operating margins are only one of the two components of the return on assets (discussed earlier in the chapter), the asset turnover ratio must also be examined.

Net Income Percentage

Net income, expressed as a percentage of sales, provides an evaluation of all current period activities. If current period sales were $500,000 and net income was $25,000, the company is earning a net profit of 5%, or 5 cents on every dollar of sales.

As a measurement device, this ratio is used by almost every reader of financial statements. Because it is easy to determine, and represents a true measurement of all the company's current period activity, it is relatively good measure.

However, since the return on shareholder equity is the important factor, once again an investor must consider this ratio in conjunction with the asset turnover ratio.

Assets Turnover

A company must have resources committed to the purchase and maintenance of business assets. Typically, it can be very costly to acquire assets if they cannot be supported by the current level of operating activity. The asset turnover ratio provides information on whether the asset base is appropriate given the sales level of the period. It is also a valuable aid in determining the assets required for anticipated business expansion. Investors should examine this ratio in conjunction with the return on assets ratio discussed earlier in the profitability ratio section.

Solvency

The third primary area of evaluation by an investor is determining the solvency of a company. The issue of solvency can be evaluated through use of the capital structure ratios.

The objective of capital structure ratios is the identification and evaluation of creditor (debt) versus ownership (equity) positions within the company. In the event of liquidation, creditors of a company have a preferential position since they are paid after employees but before stockholders. Stockholders, however, have preferential rights in the distribution of the earnings of the company via dividends.

Another reason the financial structure is important is its affect on the firm's ability to borrow additional funds or to seek new investors. If a company's debt load is considered substantial, they may not be able to acquire additional funding from creditors. Given an investor's financial interest in the company, and their second tier placement to the obligations of creditors, the debt level may also affect the ability to attract new investors or increased commitment from existing investors. Even if a company is able to attract new investors in lieu of issuing debt, it may cause a dilution of existing ownership interest.

The debt and equity mix is also important since it provides information on the future cash flow required to satisfy debt obligations. Further examination of the short term and long term debt mix put a time constraint on cash flow requirements.

A final consideration is the impact the debt and equity mix have on the calculation of the return on equity ratio. In our earlier discussion of return on equity, the impact of increased debt causing an increase in return on equity was discussed. It is important to identify the debt and equity mix in order to properly interpret the return on equity results.

Investors should use these ratios to assess the ability of a company to carry the debt level. Two capital structure ratios are helpful in answering this question. First is the debt to equity, which indicates the amount of the firm's assets presently supported by debt. The second is the times interest earned ratio. This indicates the ability of the company to service the debt. Investors should also consider the debt to equity mix as an indication of the value of the firm.

The standard ratios with their calculations are presented below.

Ratio	Calculation
Current debt to equity	$\dfrac{\text{current liabilities}}{\text{stockholder's equity}}$
Long-term debt to equity	$\dfrac{\text{long term debt}}{\text{stockholder's equity}}$
Debt to equity	$\dfrac{\text{total debt}}{\text{stockholder's equity}}$
Times interest earned	$\dfrac{\text{net income before taxes and interest}}{\text{stockholder's equity}}$

The capital structure ratios answer two common questions: how are the assets of the company financed—short term debt, long term debt or equity and can the company carry the debt level (debt to equity and times interest earned). Note that the ability to carry the debt level is determined by examining a historical perspective (i.e., the debt to equity on the Balance Sheet) as well as the current information contained in the Statement of Income. Although many investors shy away from companies with conspicuously high debt levels, high debt forces management to be efficient. If debt is high and the times interest earned ratio is not at very low levels, the advantage of leverage will be evident in a high return on equity. The primary advantages of these ratios is their ease of calculation, and their ability to summarize the often complex financial structure of a company. The disadvantage is that the results are often difficult to interpret on a relative measurement basis.

Price-Earnings Ratio

Although the ratios described in the previous pages are widely recognized and utilized, there is an additional ratio that is universally used that does not fit into the three areas of evaluation previously identified (liquidity, profitability, solvency). Because of the importance of this ratio, the price/earnings ratio (P/E), an investor must carefully consider the following discussion.

The typical investor can spend hours sorting through the Balance Sheet, Statement of Income and other financial reports to assess how well a company is managed. But is a well managed company a good investment? Not necessarily. An investor has to be able to gauge the extent to which a company's stock price fully reflects available information. The most important ratio for aiding an investor in determination of how much should be paid for the stock is the price-earnings multiple.

The price-earnings ratio, commonly referred to as the "PE multiple," can be calculated by dividing the current stock price by the earnings per share for the most recent year. What is a reasonable price-earnings multiple? There is not set answer to this question. However, a look at specific data will allow an investor to determine whether a stock is overvalued or undervalued.

Assume a company has earnings per share of $2.00 every year. If this company paid out all of its earnings as dividends, how much should an investor be willing to pay for this company's common stock? If an investor can buy this stock for $10 per share then an investor would be getting an annual return from the dividend equal to 20% of his purchase price ($2/$10 = 20%). However, if this stock was selling at $100 per share, an investor's return would be a meager 2% ($ $100 = 2%). Most investors would be very happy with an annual return of 20% and would jump at the opportunity to buy such a stock at a price of $10. The typical investor would also refuse to pay $100 for this stock as a return greater than 2% could easily be earned in another investment.

Most companies do not have the same earnings every year and do not pay out all of its earnings as dividends. A company whose earnings are growing each year will be able to pay higher dividends. Investors should be willing to pay a higher price for a company whose earnings are growing rapidly relative to a company whose earnings are growing slowly or not at all. For example, a typical, mature utility company will sell at a much lower price-earnings multiple than a company experiencing substantial percentage increase in earnings.

The average price earnings multiple for all stocks has averaged 14 over the past fifty years. At times, stocks have sold at as low a price-earnings ratio of 7 and as high as 22. It is interesting to note that when the average price earnings multiple reached 22 in 1987 the average stock declined by 40% in the subsequent months. A rough rule of thumb is that the price-earnings multiple is reasonable if it is equal to the expected long term growth rate in earnings per share.

If an investor expects a company's earnings and dividends to grow at a 25% annual rate and the current stock price is only equal to 15 times earnings per share, i.e., the PE = 15, this stock is probably a good investment at this price. However, if a stock is selling at 20 times earnings and annual growth of only 4% is expected then this stock is probably overvalued.

The attractiveness of a particular stock is a direct function of the expected growth in a company's earnings. Examining the price-earnings multiple allows an investor to determine whether the expected future earnings prospects are accurately reflected in the company's stock price. If the PE is low relative to the expected growth, then the stock is considered undervalued. If the PE is too high relative to the expected growth, the stock price is too high and it is unlikely to be a good investment.

Summary

Financial statement analysis is invaluable to an investor, and financial ratios play an integral part of such an analysis. Proper interpretation of the ratios aides in the analysis of a company's financial strengths and weaknesses. It is not simply the result of the calculation that needs interpretation, it is also the relative change from period to period.

The liquidity evaluation is designed to answer questions on the ability of a firm to meet it's obligations as they mature. Use of the standard liquidity ratios (current, quick and working capital) in conjunction with the activity ratios (receivables, inventory and payables), will enable an investor to reasonably assess a company's liquidity position.

Profitability interpretation must also be considered by an investor; although, the analysis is slightly different. In addition to a firm's profit margins (whether gross, net, or operating margins), an investor must also consider such items as asset turnover, earnings per share, return on equity and return on assets as well as the interrelationships between these evaluations. In addition, each of these elements need to be compared to industry or competitors data in order to obtain an additional perspective.

The solvency analysis completes the picture. Any increase in the debt to equity ratio is often looked upon as a negative situation. The question that must be considered is "what caused the change?" To illustrate, suppose the change was caused by a decrease in the company's common stock due to a large stock repurchase program initiated by the company. In this situation, it was not an actual increase in debt but a decline in outstanding common stock that caused the decrease.

What does this discussion on ratios mean to an investor? Simply, that an investor must use ratio analysis correctly if there is any benefit from the process. Only after the source of the change in the ratio result is identified, can an investor classify the information on a positive or negative event. In addition, investors must remember that it is critical to examine many of the ratios together in order to accurately assess the financial position and operating results of a company.

APPENDIX 1

FINANCIAL STATEMENTS OF MACK TRUCKS, INC. (1989)

Exhibit A–1

Mack Trucks, Inc.
and Consolidated Subsidiaries   **CONSOLIDATED STATEMENTS OF INCOME (LOSS)**

	Notes	1989	1988	1987
		For The Years Ended December 31		
		in thousands except per share amounts		
Revenues:				
Net sales		$1,750,734	$2,102,228	$1,857,748
Interest income		90,939	76,554	68,642
Rental income		9,281	720	40
Other		6,811	8,493	4,744
Total Revenues	1,14	1,857,765	2,187,995	1,931,174
Costs and Expenses:				
Cost of sales	1	1,736,164	1,903,220	1,700,478
Depreciation and amortization of property	1	42,202	29,619	28,249
Selling, general and administrative expenses		164,265	154,147	136,488
Interest expense	1	87,884	56,307	47,638
Provision for termination and restructuring costs	12	12,343	—	—
Total Costs and Expenses		2,042,858	2,143,293	1,912,853
Income (Loss) Before Income Taxes and Extraordinary Items		(185,093)	44,702	18,321
Provision for Income Taxes	1,10	563	19,761	13,397
Income (Loss) Before Extraordinary Items		(185,656)	24,941	4,924
Extraordinary Items	9	237	6,845	(834)
Net Income (Loss)		$ (185,419)	$ 31,786	$ 4,090
Income (Loss) Per Common and Common Equivalent Share:	16			
Income (loss) before extraordinary items		$ (6.25)	$ 0.84	$ 0.16
Extraordinary items		0.01	0.23	(0.02)
Net Income (Loss)		$ (6.24)	$ 1.07	$ 0.14

See notes to consolidated financial statements

Exhibit A–2

Mack Trucks, Inc.
and Consolidated Subsidiaries   **CONSOLIDATED BALANCE SHEETS**

Assets			December 31
	Notes	1989	1988
		in thousands	
Current Assets:			
Cash and short-term investments	4	$ **82,891**	$ 81,475
Refundable taxes		**7,362**	2,297
Trade accounts, finance and notes receivable:	1,2,3		
Accounts		**549,587**	622,193
Less unearned finance fees		**42,101**	38,700
Less allowance for uncollectible accounts		**11,787**	9,379
Trade accounts, finance and notes receivable - net		**495,699**	574,114
Inventories	1	**338,380**	393,847
Deferred income taxes	1	**—**	39,355
Prepaid expenses and other current assets		**10,219**	3,001
Total current assets		**934,551**	1,094,089
Long-Term Finance Receivables:	1,3		
Accounts		**378,012**	365,141
Less unearned finance fees		**40,675**	37,721
Less allowance for uncollectible accounts		**3,526**	3,639
Long-term finance receivables - net		**333,811**	323,781
Investments and Other Assets - net	1	**16,774**	11,428
Property - at cost	1,6,7		
Land and improvements		**24,478**	25,571
Buildings and improvements		**163,858**	165,363
Machinery and equipment		**249,343**	212,862
Motor vehicles leased to customers		**52,473**	27,558
Leased property under capital leases		**10,228**	11,074
Production model tools		**80,719**	76,411
Property - at cost		**581,099**	518,839
Less accumulated depreciation and amortization		**272,224**	255,914
Property-net		**308,875**	262,925
Intangible Assets - net	1,11	**22,208**	—
Total		**$1,616,219**	$1,692,223

Statements continued on following page

Exhibit A–3

Liabilities and Shareholders' Equity	Notes	1989	1988
		in thousands	
Current Liabilities:			
Notes payable — banks		$ 107,056	$ 44,170
Current portion of long-term debt	6,7	465,242	94,869
Accounts payable	2	132,497	157,379
Other accrued liabilities	5	202,916	189,402
Total current liabilities		907,711	485,820
Long-Term Debt:			
Notes and loans	6	315,928	594,377
Obligations under capital leases	7	6,252	7,756
Total long-term debt		322,180	602,133
Other Liabilities and Deferred Credits:			
Deferred income taxes	1	677	39,854
Deferred gain on disposal of capital assets	1	11,285	13,523
Accrued termination and restructuring costs		3,523	4,819
Other	1,11	30,228	14,892
Total other liabilities and deferred credits		45,713	73,088
Contingent Liabilities and Commitments	7,13	—	—
Redeemable Preference Shares	8	—	5,978
Shareholders' Equity:			
Common stock, par value $1 per share - authorized, 100,000,000 shares; issued, 30,714,294 and 30,594,033 shares at December 31, 1989 and 1988, respectively	2,15	30,714	30,594
Additional paid-in capital	2	318,533	317,145
Retained earnings	6	167	185,586
Equity adjustment from foreign currency translation	1	6,288	3,143
Equity adjustment — pension	1,11	(3,801)	—
		351,901	536,468
Less: Treasury stock at cost (1,018,719 and 1,016,952 shares at December 31, 1989 and 1988, respectively)		11,286	11,264
Shareholders' equity		340,615	525,204
Total		$1,616,219	$1,692,223

See notes to consolidated financial statements.

Exhibit A-4

Mack Trucks, Inc.
and Consolidated Subsidiaries　　**CONSOLIDATED STATEMENTS OF CASH FLOWS**

	For the Years Ended December 31		
	1989	1988	1987
		in thousands	
Cash Flows from Operating Activities:			
Net income (loss)	$ (185,419)	$ 31,786	$ 4,090
Adjustments to reconcile net income (loss) to net cash provided by operating activities:			
Depreciation and amortization of property	42,202	29,619	28,249
Gain on sale of assets	(6,431)	(6,097)	(2,454)
Provision for uncollectible accounts	8,905	1,919	221
Deferred income taxes & other	1,560	3,096	(1,006)
Provision for termination & restructuring costs	12,343	—	—
Changes in assets and liabilities net of foreign currency translation impact:			
Funds on deposit with trustee	(1,469)	(1,930)	(18,349)
Short-term investments	122	21,251	(9,966)
Refundable taxes	(4,968)	12,612	5,534
Trade receivables - net	62,745	(52,448)	(3,437)
Inventories	54,167	(454)	5,832
Prepaid expenses	(1,327)	2,257	(1,749)
Intangible and other assets	(23,022)	(1,985)	(3,524)
Notes payable - banks	64,365	9,868	(10,281)
Accounts payable	(27,630)	(26,236)	58,323
Accrued termination and restructuring costs	(26,461)	(37,191)	(17,523)
Other accrued liabilities	28,735	12,251	(13,846)
Other liabilities and deferred credits	14,842	3,833	(11)
Equity adjustment - pension	(3,801)	—	—
Net cash provided by operating activities	9,458	2,151	20,103
Cash Flows from Investing Activities:			
Acquisitions of finance receivables	(1,009,002)	(1,154,495)	(967,385)
Collections of finance receivables	1,010,019	1,044,843	962,765
Proceeds from sales of property	10,676	60,198	87,450
Property acquisitions	(100,479)	(102,861)	(135,875)
Investments - net	(5,765)	(223)	(1,582)
Net cash used in investing activities	(94,551)	(152,538)	(54,627)
Cash Flows from Financing Activities:			
Proceeds from issuance of long-term debt	254,828	308,343	435,561
Repayments of long-term debt	(166,613)	(126,549)	(416,801)
Issuance of common stock	1,508	827	1,363
Purchase of treasury stock	(22)	(94)	(171)
Redemption of preference shares	(5,805)	—	(3,365)
Net cash provided by financing activities	83,896	182,527	16,587
Effect of exchange rate changes on cash	1,266	(1,911)	(526)
Net increase (decrease) in cash	69	30,229	(18,463)
Cash at beginning of the year	42,921	12,692	31,155
Cash at end of the year	$ 42,990	$ 42,921	$ 12,692
Supplemental Disclosures of Cash Flow Information:			
Cash paid during the year for:			
Interest - net of amount capitalized	$ 84,244	$ 54,661	$ 48,096
Income taxes paid (refunded)	$ (2,183)	$ 2,916	$ 2,502

See notes to consolidated financial statements

Exhibit A–5

Mack Trucks, Inc.
and Consolidated Subsidiaries

CONSOLIDATED STATEMENTS OF CHANGES IN SHAREHOLDERS' EQUITY

	Number of Shares		Common Stock	Additional Paid-In Capital	Retained Earnings	Cumulative Foreign Currency Adjustments	Equity Adjustment Pension	Treasury Stock
	Common Stock	Treasury Stock						
Balance, December 31, 1986	30,423,225	1,000,000	$30,423	$315,126	$149,710	$(13,778)	$ —	$ (10,999)
Net income					4,090			
Issuance of shares under stock option and award plan · net	104,488		104	1,259				
Foreign currency translation adjustment						6,445		
Purchase of treasury stock		9,958						(171)
Balance, December 31, 1987	30,527,713	1,009,958	30,527	316,385	153,800	(7,333)	—	(11,170)
Net income					31,786			
Issuance of shares under stock option and award plan · net	66,320		67	760				
Foreign currency translation adjustment						10,476		
Purchase of treasury stock		6,994						(94)
Balance, December 31, 1988	30,594,033	1,016,952	30,594	317,145	185,586	3,143	—	(11,264)
Net loss					(185,419)			
Issuance of shares under stock option and award plan · net	120,261		120	1,388				
Foreign currency translation adjustment						3,145		
Pension adjustment							(3,801)	
Purchase of treasury stock		1,767						(22)
Balance, December 31, 1989	30,714,294	1,018,719	$30,714	$318,533	$ 167	$ 6,288	$ (3,801)	$(11,286)

dollars in thousands

See notes to consolidated financial statements.

Exhibit A–6

Mack Trucks, Inc.
and Consolidated Subsidiaries

NOTES TO CONSOLIDATED FINANCIAL STATEMENTS
For the Years Ended December 31, 1989, 1988 and 1987

1. Summary of Significant Accounting Policies

Basis of Presentation

The Company's consolidated financial statements have been presented on a going concern basis which contemplates the realization of assets and the satisfaction of liabilities in the normal course of business. As more fully described under "Management's Discussion and Analysis of Results of Operations and Financial Condition" and in Note 6 below, the liquidity of the Company has been adversely affected during 1989 by significant losses from operations. The Company and all its U.S. bank lenders have reached an agreement on the principal terms for the consolidation of the Company's outstanding U.S. bank debt into a three-year syndicated secured credit agreement, subject to agreement on final documentation and the purchase of $50 million of subordinated debt by its major shareholder, Renault Vehicules Industriels ("RVI"). RVI has agreed to purchase $50 million of convertible subordinated debentures, subject to certain conditions including the execution of the new bank credit agreement and satisfactory renegotiation of bank credit agreements of certain of the Company's subsidiaries.

The Company believes that execution of the above agreements will provide sufficient liquidity for it to continue as a going concern in its present form. Accordingly, the consolidated financial statements do not include any adjustments relating to the recoverability and classification of recorded asset amounts or the amount and classification of liabilities or any other adjustments that might be necessary should the Company be unable to continue as a going concern in its present form.

Principles of Consolidation

The accompanying consolidated financial statements include the accounts of the Company and all majority-owned subsidiaries. Intercompany accounts and transactions have been eliminated in consolidation.

Foreign Currency Translation

Transaction gains and losses, resulting from exchange rate changes on transactions denominated in currencies other than that of the Company's foreign subsidiaries, are generally included in income in the year in which the change occurs.

The Company recorded a transaction loss of $262,000 in 1989, and gains of $1,857,000 and $378,000 in 1988 and 1987, respectively.

Finance Receivables

Finance receivables are comprised of retail instalment receivables and customer truck accounts receivable from the sale and lease of new and used motor vehicles and wholesale (floor plan) receivables from the financing of distributors' inventories.

Finance fees, included in retail instalment receivables, are taken into income over the lives of the contracts. Interest and service charges from distributors on wholesale notes receivable and certain other interest-bearing receivables are recorded as earned based on the outstanding balances.

Exhibit A–7

1. Summary of Significant Accounting Policies continued

Inventories

Inventories of finished units (new and used) and service parts are stated at the lower of cost or selling price (after allowance for selling expenses). Raw materials and work in process are stated at cost which is not in excess of replacement market. It is impractical to segregate inventories of raw materials from work in process. Intercompany profits have been eliminated from inventories. The inventory values at year-end were as follows:

	1989	1988
	in thousands	
Finished units (new and used)	$153,266	$189,985
Service parts	99,174	110,612
Raw materials and work in process	85,940	93,250
Total inventories at December 31	$338,380	$393,847

For substantially all domestic inventories, cost was determined by the last-in, first-out (LIFO) method. The cost of inventories outside of the United States was determined generally by the average cost method. If the average cost method had been used for all inventories in 1989 and 1988, inventories would have been increased by approximately $91,450,000 and $89,567,000 at December 31, 1989 and 1988, respectively.

During 1989, 1988, and 1987, reductions of inventory quantities resulted in liquidations of LIFO inventories carried at costs prevailing in prior years which were different from current costs. The effects of these reductions were as follows:

	1989	1988	1987
	in thousands		
LIFO inventory liquidated	$ 25,832	$24,629	$10,966
Increase (reduction) of cost of sales	$ (11,550)	$ (9,448)	$ 119
Increase (reduction) of net income	$ 11,550	$ 5,801	$ (66)

Property, Depreciation and Amortization

Depreciation and amortization of property are provided over the following estimated service lives:

Land improvements	25 years
Buildings and improvements	20 to 40 years; terms of leases as to leasehold improvements
Machinery and equipment	3 to 20 years
Motor vehicles leased to customers	Terms of leases (generally 2 to 5 years)
Production model tools, etc.	5 to 10 years

In general, the declining balance method of computing depreciation and amortization is used for property. The straight-line method of computing depreciation and amortization is used for leased vehicles, property acquired prior to 1973 in connection with the Company's Hagerstown plant, and other property acquired prior to 1954. Assets recorded under capital leases are amortized generally over the terms of the leases under methods which are consistent with the Company's normal depreciation policy for owned assets.

Maintenance, repairs and renewals of a minor nature are charged to expense as incurred. Renewals of a major nature and improvements are capitalized.

Exhibit A–8

Mack Trucks, Inc.
and Consolidated Subsidiaries   **NOTES TO CONSOLIDATED FINANCIAL STATEMENTS**

1. Summary of Significant Accounting Policies continued

Leases	The Company's leasing agreements (see Note 7) consist of three general types of arrangements. The Company leases certain equipment at two locations under the terms of sale-leaseback agreements classified as operating leases with terms ranging from seven to eighteen years. The deferred gains on the sales of the assets are amortized on a straight-line basis over the lease terms. The agreements contain purchase options available to the Company. In the normal course of business, the Company leases computer equipment and facilities throughout the United States, Canada and Australia to support its operations. The lease agreements covering this equipment and facilities are classified as either capital or operating leases as appropriate. Lastly, the Company leases motor vehicles to customers under operating leases, generally for periods of three to five years.
Investments	Investments are recorded at net realizable value.
Deferred Expenses	The deferred debt expense included in other assets is being amortized over the terms of the issues.
Product Warranty Costs	Provision for estimated costs related to product warranties is made at the time the products are sold.
Research and Development Costs	Expenditures for research and development are charged to expense as incurred and amounted to $27,029,000 in 1989, $26,247,000 in 1988, and $26,174,000 in 1987.
Interest Costs	Capitalized interest costs amounted to $3,584,000, $5,922,000, and $1,889,000 in 1989, 1988, and 1987, respectively.
Income Taxes	Deferred income taxes result from timing differences between accounting for financial statement purposes and accounting for income tax purposes (see Note 10). During the fourth quarter of 1989, the Company eliminated all deferred income taxes related to its U.S. operations due to the loss carryforward position created by the large net loss incurred by such operations. No provision has been made for U.S. income taxes on unremitted earnings of subsidiaries as to which U.S. federal income taxes payable upon distribution would be substantially offset by foreign tax credits. Statement of Financial Accounting Standards No. 96, ''Accounting for Income Taxes'' (FAS 96), issued in December 1987, requires deferred taxes to be recorded based on the tax rate at which they are expected to be settled. FAS 103, issued in December 1989, deferred the effective date of FAS 96 until 1992, the year the Company plans to implement FAS 96. The Company will not apply FAS 96 retroactively and anticipates that, in the year of adoption, this change in accounting principle will not materially affect net income.
Reclassification and Accounting Changes	Effective January 1, 1989, the Company was required to adopt the additional minimum liability and non-U.S. pension plan provisions of Statement of Financial Accounting Standards No. 87, ''Employers' Accounting for Pensions.'' The additional minimum liability provision pertains only to underfunded defined benefit pension plans. Accordingly, an additional minimum liability of $22,793,000, an intangible asset of $18,992,000 and an equity reduction of $3,801,000 were recorded at December 31, 1989. See Note 11. Certain amounts in the accompanying financial statements for the years ended December 31, 1988 and 1987, have been reclassified to conform with 1989 classifications.

Exhibit A–9

2. Relationship with Renault

As of December 31, 1989, Regie Nationale des Usines Renault ("Renault"), through its wholly-owned subsidiary, Renault Vehicles Industriels S.A. ("RVI"), owned 13,250,000 shares of the Company's common stock. RVI also owns a warrant, which expires in 1998, to purchase 5,034,160 shares of Mack common stock at $14.7143 per share, after antidilution adjustments, and holds an option to purchase additional shares from the Company from time to time to maintain its equity interest in the Company. Subsequent to December 31, 1989 (see Note 18), the Company and RVI reached an agreement in principle, on the terms of $50,000,000 of convertible subordinated debentures. The debentures bear an interest rate of 8% and have a term of 20 years, with repayments beginning after 10 years. The debentures may be converted at any time into 7,009,550 shares of the Company's common stock (subject to antidilution adjustments). If the debenture is converted, RVI would own 55.1% of the Company's common stock.

The Company is the exclusive distributor in the United States, Canada and certain Central American and Caribbean countries of Class 6 and Class 7 medium-duty diesel trucks manufactured by RVI. The Company's unit sales of RVI vehicles were 4,539 in 1989, 5,696 in 1988, and 5,968 in 1987.

During the three years ended December 31, 1989, the following transactions by the Company, and the year-end balances between the Company and Renault have been reflected in the financial statements:

	1989	1988	1987
		in thousands	
Purchases of medium-duty trucks and service parts	$140,614	$155,476	$134,701
Interest earned on investments	$ —	$ —	$ 339
Interest paid on short-term notes	$ —	$ —	$ 536
Sales of engines and parts	$ 2,118	$ 1,597	$ 1,201
Accounts receivable (including interest on investments)	$ 3,159	$ 1,348	$ 1,815
Trade accounts payable	$ 20,262	$ 19,776	$ 31,063

3. Financial and Leasing Subsidiaries

The Company has three wholly-owned financial and leasing subsidiaries — Mack Financial Corporation and subsidiaries (MFC), Mack Finance Australia Pty. Ltd. and Mack Americus, Inc. The combined results of operations for the financial and leasing subsidiaries, prior to consolidation, were as follows:

	For the Years Ended December 31		
	1989	1988	1987
		in thousands	
Interest and rental income	$ 116,231	$ 89,285	$ 76,750
Expenses:			
Interest and debt expense	72,111	50,915	37,257
Provision (credit) for uncollectible accounts	4,196	250	(1,088)
Other operating expenses	19,104	13,382	11,406
Total	95,411	64,547	47,575
Income from operations	20,820	24,738	29,175
Provision for income taxes	7,589	9,562	12,499
Income before extraordinary item	13,231	15,176	16,676
Extraordinary item (net of tax benefit)	—	—	(1,120)
Net income	13,231	15,176	15,556
Retained earnings at beginning of year	99,226	84,050	168,494
Total	112,457	99,226	184,050
Less dividends	—	—	100,000
Retained earnings at end of year	$112,457	$ 99,226	$ 84,050

Exhibit A–10

Mack Trucks, Inc.
and Consolidated Subsidiaries   **NOTES TO CONSOLIDATED FINANCIAL STATEMENTS**

**3. Financial and
Leasing Subsidiaries**
continued

The combined financial condition of the financial and leasing subsidiaries, prior to consolidation, was as follows:

	December 31	
	1989	1988
Assets	in thousands	
Cash	$ 34,504	$ 17,962
Funds on deposit with trustee - See Note 4	21,748	20,279
Trade receivables	36,478	34,383
Finance receivables	805,375	827,491
Less unearned finance fees	82,776	76,421
Less allowance for uncollectible accounts	8,021	7,594
Finance receivables - net	714,578	743,476
Other receivables	4,496	2,184
Inventory of repossessions - net	6,698	5,214
Motor vehicles leased to customers - net	39,144	25,064
Other assets and deferred charges	2,749	2,074
Total	$860,395	$850,636

	December 31	
	1989	1988
Liabilities and Shareholder's Equity	in thousands	
Short-term notes payable - banks	$ 10,000	$ 25,000
Other liabilities and deferred credits	14,480	13,965
Due to Mack Trucks, Inc. and subsidiary	40,237	55,313
Long-term debt	653,804	628,893
Shareholder's equity		
Common stock	25,000	25,000
Additional paid-in capital	1,700	1,700
Retained earnings	112,457	99,226
Equity adjustment from foreign currency translation	2,717	1,539
Total shareholder's equity	141,874	127,465
Total	$860,395	$850,636

Total assets at December 31, 1989, include $215,389,000 of assets owned by Mack Trucks Receivables Corporation (MTRC), a wholly-owned, limited-purpose subsidiary of MFC. Such assets include $21,748,000 of funds on deposit with trustee (see Note 4) and $183,962,000 of finance receivables, net of unearned finance fees, which collateralize outstanding Truck Receivables Underlying Certificates (TRUCS℠), which are solely the obligations of MTRC (see Note 6).

More information about MFC is available in MFC's 1989 Annual Report, which may be obtained by writing to MFC, Box M, Allentown, PA 18105-5000.

Exhibit A–11

4. Cash & Short-Term Investments

Cash and short-term investments at year-end (stated at cost, which equals market value) were as follows:

	1989	1988
	in thousands	
Cash	$42,990	$ 42,921
Funds on deposit with trustee	21,748	20,279
Short-term investments	18,153	18,275
Total	$82,891	$ 81,475

Funds on deposit with trustee represent monies collected from retail instalment finance receivables. These funds are restricted to the extent necessary to satisfy the debt service requirements of the TRUCS[SM] Notes and certain operating costs of Mack Trucks Receivables Corporation (MTRC), a wholly-owned, limited-purpose subsidiary of MFC (see Note 6). Short-term investments consist of time deposits with terms ranging up to three months.

5. Other Accrued Liabilities

Other accrued liabilities at year-end consisted of:

	1989	1988
	in thousands	
Accrued warranty	$ 71,795	$ 52,484
Accrued liabilities to distributors	50,393	35,652
Accrued wages and commissions	21,387	23,826
Other accrued liabilities	59,341	77,440
Total	$202,916	$189,402

6. Long-Term Notes, Loans Payable and Credit Arrangements

At December 31, 1989, the Company and MFC had received waivers of defaults that arose under a number of bank loan agreements as a result of the Company's failure to maintain specified financial ratios. The Company has received waivers, extended through April 15, 1990, of the relevant covenants and related provisions, by virtue of which MFC is not currently in default under its loan agreements. There can be no assurances that any of such waivers will be extended beyond April 15, if necessary, in the event that the Credit Agreement, below, is not executed by then. The amount of principal as to which the Company and MFC have received waivers was $384.3 million at December 31, 1989.

The Company and all its U.S. bank lenders have reached an agreement on the principal terms of a three-year syndicated secured credit agreement (the "Credit Agreement") under which the Company's bank borrowings of $143,250,000 would be consolidated into a three-year term facility bearing interest at 1.5% above the agent bank's alternate base rate and with amortization beginning after 18 months. The Credit Agreement includes a $5 million letter of credit facility and will also permit the Company to establish a revolving credit facility in a maximum amount of $50 million. The Company's ability to borrow under the revolving credit facility would depend on the levels of the borrowing base (as defined in the Credit Agreement) and the amount of debt or equity issued by the Company after the Credit Agreement's effective date. Security for the Credit Agreement would include the Company's inventory and the shares of stock of certain subsidiaries. While the Company does not expect that on the Credit Agreement's effective date any lenders will have agreed to provide credit under the revolving credit facility, the Company intends to seek institutions to provide such credit. The Credit Agreement contains covenants relating to, among other things, maintenance of a specified current ratio, and the sum of the Company's cumulative net income (loss) plus the proceeds of any future issue of subordinated debt or equity by the Company. Under the Credit Agreement, the Company would not be permitted to pay any dividends (other than stock dividends) on its common stock. Execution of the Credit Agreement is subject to agreement on final documentation and the purchase of $50 million of subordinated debt by RVI.

Exhibit A-12

Mack Trucks, Inc.
and Consolidated Subsidiaries

NOTES TO CONSOLIDATED FINANCIAL STATEMENTS

6. Long-Term Notes, Loans Payable and Credit Arrangements
continued

Additionally, the Company has entered into an agreement in principle with RVI, under which, subject to certain conditions (including execution of the Credit Agreement and satisfactory renegotiations of bank credit agreements of certain of the Company's subsidiaries), RVI will purchase $50 million of the Company's 8% convertible subordinated debentures having a term of 20 years, convertible at any time into 7,009,550 shares of the Company's common stock (subject to antidilution adjustments). The proceeds of such purchase, as well as borrowings that may become available under the revolving credit facility, will be used for the funding of further losses and the Company's anticipated liquidity and other financing needs.

Long-term notes and loans payable at year-end consisted of:

	1989	1988
	in thousands	
Revolving credit loans pursuant to a revolving credit agreement of Mack Financial Corporation (MFC) expiring in July 1990 (the weighted average interest rate in effect at December 31, 1989 was 9.89%)	$306,000	$ —
10.9% Note due in four semiannual instalments of $1,250,000 commencing September 1988, followed by one instalment of $5,000,000 in September 1990	6,250	8,750
Financial facilities of Mack Trucks Australia Pty. Ltd., expiring in June 1991 (interest at 1% above the bank's prime rate; at December 31, 1989, the interest rate in effect was 19.58%)	9,474	10,248
10% Note of Mack Americus, Inc. due in December 1991	40,000	—
TRUCS℠ Series 1 Class 1-B 8.05% Notes of Mack Trucks Receivables Corporation (MTRC), due in quarterly instalments ending in June 1992	20,822	65,410
Revolving credit loans pursuant to a revolving credit agreement of Mack Americus, Inc. expiring in 1992 (the weighted average interest rate in effect at December 31, 1989 was 9.18%)	35,000	50,000
TRUCS℠ Series 2 Class 2-B 8.35% Notes of MTRC, due in quarterly instalments ending in May 1993	49,984	74,555
TRUCS℠ Series 3 10.2% Notes of MTRC, due in quarterly instalments ending in March 1994	103,330	—
Revolving credit loans pursuant to various revolving credit agreements expiring in 1990, 1991 and 1994 (the weighted average interest rate in effect at December 31, 1989 was 9.28%)	67,000	—
Revolving credit loans pursuant to various revolving credit agreements of Mack Financial (Canada), Ltd. expiring in 1991, 1992 and 1994 (net of unamortized discount of $1,124,000 and $999,000 at December 31, 1989 and 1988, respectively; the weighted average interest rate in effect at December 31, 1989 was 12.41%)	98,668	97,047
7-7/8% sinking fund debentures, due in annual instalments of $3,750,000 through September 1997 ($146,000 and $3,831,000 in total principal amount redeemed in advance at December 31, 1989 and 1988, respectively)	29,854	29,919
Mortgage notes, due through 2008 - annual interest rates ranging from .875% to 13.0%	13,789	10,415
TRUCS℠ Series 2 Class 2-A 7.45% Notes of MTRC, due in quarterly instalments ending in May 1989	—	19,881
Competitive advance facility loans pursuant to a competitive advance credit agreement of MFC expiring in July 1990	—	322,000
Total	780,171	688,225
Less current portion	464,243	93,848
Long-term portion	$315,928	$594,377

The Truck Receivables Underlying Certificates (TRUCS℠), which are obligations solely of MTRC, are secured by retail instalment finance receivables which were sold by MFC to MTRC concurrently with the issuance of the TRUCS and which are serviced by MFC.

The competitive advance facility and revolving credit loans of MFC and Mack Americus, Inc. are secured by finance receivables held and serviced by MFC. Mortgage notes are secured by the value of the underlying property.

Exhibit A–13

6. Long-Term Notes, Loans Payable and Credit Arrangements
continued

At December 31, 1989, certain of the Company's consolidated subsidiaries had $40,916,000 of unused availability under the terms of revolving credit agreements and general lines of credit with several banks. Amounts borrowed under these agreements bear interest generally at money market rates. Borrowings under the revolving credit agreements could be repaid on a short-term basis or converted to term loans. The Company is required to pay a commitment fee of up to 0.5% annually on the unused portion of the revolving credit agreements. These agreements are subject to annual review and to the maintenance of financial condition satisfactory to the banks.

As of December 31, 1989, maturities of long-term debt for the five years ending December 31, 1990 through 1994, were as follows: $464,243,000 (classified as a current liability at December 31, 1989), $135,432,000, $112,900,000, $9,957,000, and $39,814,000.

The long-term debt agreements contain, among other matters, provisions relative to additional borrowings, maintenance of working capital, restrictions on the amounts of investments, loans or advances, and restrictions on the amount of retained earnings available for the payment of dividends. Under the most restrictive of these agreements, no retained earnings at December 31, 1989, were available for the payment of dividends.

7. Leases

Lease commitments payable at December 31, 1989, under capital leases and non-cancelable operating leases with an initial term of more than one year were as follows:

	Capital Leases	Operating Leases
	in thousands	
1990	$ 2,509	$ 22,501
1991	1,995	19,783
1992	1,579	19,580
1993	1,463	20,080
1994	1,463	13,950
Later years	9,131	124,697
Total	$ 18,140	$ 220,591
Less: Estimated executory costs (such as taxes, maintenance and insurance) and profit thereon	4,544	
Amount representing interest	6,345	
Present value of minimum lease payments	7,251	
Less current portion	999	
Present value of noncurrent portion of obligations under capital leases	$ 6,252	

(Future Minimum Lease and Rental Payments)

Future minimum lease payments have not been reduced by future minimum sublease rentals of $721,000.

Leased property under capital leases, by major classifications, at December 31, 1989 and 1988, was as follows:

	1989	1988
	in thousands	
Land and buildings	$ 6,975	$ 7,824
Machinery and equipment	3,253	3,250
Total	10,228	11,074
Less accumulated amortization	6,490	5,730
Leased property—net	$ 3,738	$ 5,344

Total rent expense charged to income under operating leases amounted to approximately $26,864,000 in 1989, $20,675,000 in 1988, and $16,268,000 in 1987.

Exhibit A–14

Mack Trucks, Inc.
and Consolidated Subsidiaries

NOTES TO CONSOLIDATED FINANCIAL STATEMENTS

7. Leases continued

Future rentals receivable at December 31, 1989, under noncancelable motor vehicle operating leases were as follows:

	Future Minimum Rental Receipts
	in thousands
1990	$ 11,541
1991	11,170
1992	6,002
1993	1,376
1994	345
Total	$30,434

As of December 31, 1989, motor vehicles leased to customers under operating leases and motor vehicles held for lease are stated at a cost of $52,473,000 less accumulated depreciation of $9,626,000.

8. Redeemable Preference Shares

The redeemable preference shares represented securities issued by Mack Trucks Australia Pty. Ltd., the Company's wholly-owned Australian subsidiary. The shares were redeemed, as scheduled, on February 8, 1989.

9. Extraordinary Items

The extraordinary items consisted of the following:

	For The Years Ended December 31		
	1989	1988	1987
	in thousands		
Tax benefits	$ 237	$6,845	$ 286
Early redemption premiums - net	—	—	(1,120)
Total extraordinary items	$ 237	$6,845	$ (834)

Tax benefits are the benefits associated with operating expenses included in prior years, for which tax benefits could not then be recorded. The early redemption premiums are premiums incurred by Mack Financial Corporation on the early redemption of four issues of Senior Notes and Debentures and two issues of Senior Subordinated Notes. The tax benefits associated with the early redemption premiums were $862,000.

10. Income Taxes

The provision (credit) for income taxes for the years ended December 31, 1989, 1988, and 1987, consisted of the following:

	Current	Deferred	Total
	in thousands		
1989:			
United States	$ 606	$ (633)	$ (27)
State	864	(153)	711
Foreign	(146)	25	(121)
Total	1,324	(761)	563
1988:			
United States	(768)	7,297	6,529
State	656	69	725
Foreign	11,737	770	12,507
Total	11,625	8,136	19,761
1987:			
United States	3,594	(2,784)	810
State	2,038	(62)	1,976
Foreign	9,683	928	10,611
Total	$ 15,315	$ (1,918)	$ 13,397

Exhibit A–15

10. Income Taxes
continued

The tax effect of the various timing differences and other changes entering into the provision (credit) for deferred income taxes follows:

	1989	1988	1987
	in thousands		
Tax NOL and credit carryforwards	$ (56,691)	$ (9,100)	$ —
Adjustment of deferred taxes due to loss carryforwards	54,741	(4,273)	267
Accrued termination and restructuring costs	7,981	17,254	4,720
Warranty	(4,847)	(572)	717
Early retirement program	—	7,145	6,456
Depreciation	1,922	2,283	2,341
TRAC leasing	(1,889)	1,395	176
Inventory capitalization adjustment	(1,657)	(1,193)	(1,039)
Sale and leaseback transactions	848	(137)	(9,747)
Intercompany profit in inventory	(485)	1,512	(26)
Instalment sales	(236)	(5,565)	(571)
Health care retention accrual	(198)	(318)	(3,931)
Accrued legal claims	172	(912)	(1,682)
Other	(422)	617	401
Total deferred income tax provision (credit)	$ (761)	$ 8,136	$ (1,918)

Income (loss) before income taxes and extraordinary items consisted of the following:

	1989	1988	1987
	in thousands		
United States	$ (184,151)	$17,366	$ 928
Foreign	(942)	27,336	17,393
Total	$ (185,093)	$44,702	$18,321

A reconciliation between the provision (credit) for income taxes computed by applying the statutory U.S. federal income tax rate to income (loss) before income taxes and extraordinary items, and the actual provision (credit) for income taxes follows:

	1989	1988	1987
	in thousands		
Income tax (credit) at U.S. federal statutory rate	$ (62,932)	$ 15,199	$ 7,328
Effect of nonrecognition of tax benefits on expenses recorded but deductible in future tax years	55,707	—	720
Tax effect of a distribution of capital of a consolidated foreign subsidiary	7,341	—	—
State income taxes net of federal income tax benefit	470	467	1,154
Foreign tax rate differential	75	4,128	3,790
Other	(98)	(33)	405
Total provision (credit) for income taxes	$ 563	$ 19,761	$ 13,397

At December 31, 1989, the Company had an estimated $150 million of U.S. net operating loss (NOL) carryforwards available to reduce future taxable income. For financial reporting purposes, the Company had a total U.S. NOL carryforward of $256 million recorded at December 31, 1989, to reduce financial income. The $106 million difference arises primarily as a result of the timing of recognition of expenses for financial and tax purposes. The amount of carryforwards available to reduce future taxable income expires in the years 2000 through 2004.

The Company also has various domestic tax credit carryforwards aggregating $11 million at December 31, 1989, scheduled to expire in the years 1992 through 2003.

11. Post Retirement Benefits

The Company and its subsidiaries sponsor defined benefit retirement income plans covering substantially all bargaining and non-bargaining employees, including certain employees in foreign countries. Although benefits are based on years of credited service, non-bargaining employees have a contributory option providing benefits with a pay-related formula. The Company's policy is to fund amounts as are necessary to at least meet the minimum funding requirements of ERISA.

Retirement plan assets are invested primarily in listed equity securities, corporate debt securities and governmental obligations. Included in plan assets are 1,000,000 shares of the Company's common stock.

Exhibit A–16

Mack Trucks, Inc.
and Consolidated Subsidiaries

NOTES TO CONSOLIDATED FINANCIAL STATEMENTS

11. Post Retirement Benefits
continued

Effective January 1, 1989, the Company was required to adopt the additional minimum liability provision of Statement of Financial Accounting Standards No. 87, "Employers' Accounting for Pensions" (FAS 87). Also, the defined benefit retirement income plans of the Company's Canadian subsidiary are now required to be accounted for in accordance with FAS 87.

Net pension expense (income) included the following components:

	1989	1988	1987
	in thousands		
Service cost-benefits earned during the period	$ 5,691	$ 5,401	$ 8,062
Interest cost on projected benefit obligation	37,785	36,384	36,906
Actual return on assets	(70,071)	(43,630)	(7,543)
Net amortization and deferral	26,066	3,438	(34,317)
Net pension expense (income)	$ (529)	$ 1,593	$ 3,108

Additionally, in 1987, there was a net gain of $5,101,000 resulting from the layoff of a significant number of employees in that year. Also, a special early retirement program was offered to domestic employees meeting certain age and service requirements in 1987. The cost of this 1987 program, $12,537,000, was provided for as part of a charge for termination and restructuring costs in a prior year.

The following table sets forth the funded status of the retirement income plans and the amounts recognized in the Company's consolidated balance sheets at December 31, 1989 and 1988:

	1989		1988	
	in thousands			
	Assets Exceed Accumulated Benefits	Accumulated Benefits Exceed Assets	Assets Exceed Accumulated Benefits	Accumulated Benefits Exceed Assets
Actuarial present value of benefit obligations:				
Vested benefit obligation	$ 96,317	$ 267,622	$ 84,788	$ 257,072
Accumulated benefit obligation	$ 112,069	$ 317,117	$ 99,141	$ 296,951
Projected benefit obligation	$ 116,980	$ 317,117	$ 103,156	$ 296,951
Plan assets at fair value	147,454	304,266	116,478	277,545
Projected benefit obligation (in excess of) less than plan assets	30,474	(12,851)	13,322	(19,406)
Unrecognized net loss	7,319	18,190	9,698	19,515
Unrecognized net transition asset	(34,174)	(14,389)	(29,605)	(15,782)
Unrecognized prior service cost	356	18,992	350	20,718
Additional minimum liability	—	(22,793)	—	—
Prepaid pension asset (liability)	$ 3,975	$ (12,851)	$ (6,235)	$ 5,045

One domestic retirement income plan is in an underfunded position at December 31, 1989. An additional minimum liability is required to recognize this underfunded position. An intangible asset equal to the unrecognized prior service cost is also recorded. Since the additional minimum liability exceeds the unrecognized prior service cost, the excess is reported as a reduction of equity.

Domestic projected benefit obligations at December 31, 1989, were determined using a discount rate of 9% and a rate of increase in compensation of 6% (9.5% and 7% at December 31, 1988, respectively). The expected long-term rate of return on domestic plan assets is 10.5%.

The Company also contributes to several domestic multiemployer retirement income plans which provide benefits to certain employees. Pension expense and contributions to such plans amounted to $353,000, $359,000, and $409,000 for 1989, 1988, and 1987, respectively.

In addition to providing pension benefits, the Company provides health care and life insurance benefits for retired employees. The Company recognizes the cost of providing these benefits by expensing the actual claims. The cost of providing these benefits for retirees of U.S. operations is estimated at $23,700,000, $20,300,000, and $15,900,000 for 1989, 1988, and 1987, respectively.

Exhibit A-17

12. Provision for Termination and Restructuring Costs

The $12,343,000 provision for termination and restructuring costs recorded in 1989 includes the estimated costs associated with employees terminated in 1989, the planned termination of certain Company-owned sales branches, and an additional provision for the 1985 termination of the Company's Allentown, PA assembly operations.

13. Contingent Liabilities

The Company is a party to a number of lawsuits and is subject to various claims arising in the ordinary course of its business, the outcome of which, in the opinion of the Company's management, should not have a material adverse effect on the financial position of the Company and its subsidiaries taken as a whole.

At December 31, 1989, the Company was contingently liable for approximately $2,500,000 for the repurchase of distributor parts inventories.

14. Business Segments

The Company's and its consolidated subsidiaries' operations are principally related to the truck manufacturing and financing and leasing industries. Truck operations involve the manufacture and sale of heavy-duty trucks, truck tractors and truck replacement parts and the providing of repair and maintenance service for such products. The Company also is a distributor of medium-duty diesel trucks and busses manufactured by R.V.I. (see Note 2). Financing and leasing operations involve financing retail and wholesale receivables, and the leasing of motor vehicles to customers.

Operations of the Company and its consolidated subsidiaries are conducted primarily in the United States, Canada and Australia. Revenue by geographic area and industry segments includes sales to unaffiliated customers, as reported in the consolidated statements of income (loss), and transfers between segments which are accounted for on the basis of negotiated prices. Income (loss) before extraordinary items for each segment is based upon the financial statements of such segments including income resulting from transfers between the segments. Segment information about the operations of the Company and its consolidated subsidiaries is summarized below:

	United States	Canada	Australia	Adjustment	Consolidated
1989:			in millions		
Revenues:					
Truck Operations:					
Net sales to customers	$1,474.7	$ 171.3	$104.8	$ —	$1,750.8
Transfers between geographical areas	134.6	87.3	—	(221.9)	—
Total net sales	1,609.3	258.6	104.8	(221.9)	1,750.8
Interest income	4.5	2.4	.4	(3.9)	3.4
Other revenue	6.6	(.1)	.3	—	6.8
Total	$1,620.4	$260.9	$105.5	$ (225.8)	$1,761.0
Financial and Leasing Subsidiaries					
Interest and rental income	$ 78.3	$ 18.3	$ .2	$ —	$ 96.8
Transfers between segments	16.4	2.6	—	(19.0)	—
Total	$ 94.7	$ 20.9	$ .2	$ (19.0)	$ 96.8
Total Revenues	$1,715.1	$281.8	$105.7	$ (244.8)	$1,857.8
Income (loss) before extraordinary items - truck operations	$ (195.3)	$ (3.1)	$ .4	$ (.9)	$ (198.9)
Income before extraordinary items - financial and leasing subsidiaries	10.5	2.7	—	—	13.2
Income (loss) before extraordinary items	$ (184.8)	$ (.4)	$ .4	$ (.9)	$ (185.7)
Identifiable assets at December 31, 1989:					
Truck Operations	$ 713.6	$ 66.9	$ 59.3	$ (84.0)	$ 755.8
Financial and Leasing Subsidiaries	714.0	145.3	1.1	—	860.4
Total	$1,427.6	$212.2	$ 60.4	$ (84.0)	$1,616.2

Exhibit A–18

Mack Trucks, Inc.
and Consolidated Subsidiaries

NOTES TO CONSOLIDATED FINANCIAL STATEMENTS

14. Business Segments continued

	United States	Canada	Australia	Adjustment	Consolidated
1988:			in millions		
Revenues:					
Truck Operations:					
Net sales to customers	$1,730.2	$254.0	$118.0	$ —	$2,102.2
Transfers between geographical areas	146.2	96.9	—	(243.1)	—
Total net sales	1,876.4	350.9	118.0	(243.1)	2,102.2
Interest income	4.3	2.7	.3	(2.6)	4.7
Other revenue	7.9	.3	.3	—	8.5
Total	$1,888.6	$353.9	$118.6	$(245.7)	$2,115.4
Financial and Leasing Subsidiaries:					
Interest and rental income	$ 56.6	$ 15.7	$ .3	$ —	$ 72.6
Transfers between segments	13.4	3.1	—	(16.5)	—
Total	$ 70.0	$ 18.8	$ .3	$ (16.5)	$ 72.6
Total Revenues	$1,958.6	$372.7	$118.9	$(262.2)	$2,188.0
Income (loss) before extraordinary items - truck operations	$ (2.6)	$ 12.7	$ (.8)	$ .5	$ 9.8
Income before extraordinary items - financial and leasing subsidiaries	12.4	2.7	—	—	15.1
Income (loss) before extraordinary items	$ 9.8	$ 15.4	$ (.8)	$ .5	$ 24.9
Identifiable assets at December 31, 1988:					
Truck Operations	$ 716.3	$ 77.4	$ 54.4	$ (6.4)	$ 841.7
Financial and Leasing Subsidiaries	674.1	174.5	1.9	—	850.5
Total	$1,390.4	$251.9	$ 56.3	$ (6.4)	$1,692.2
1987:					
Revenues:					
Truck Operations:					
Net sales to customers	$1,556.0	$238.8	$62.9	$ —	$1,857.7
Transfers between geographical areas	113.9	33.4	—	(147.3)	—
Total net sales	1,669.9	272.2	62.9	(147.3)	1,857.7
Interest income	4.6	2.0	.5	(1.9)	5.2
Other revenue	4.1	.3	.4	—	4.8
Total	$1,678.6	$274.5	$63.8	$(149.2)	$1,867.7
Financial and Leasing Subsidiaries:					
Interest and rental income	$ 50.4	$ 12.8	$ .3	$ —	$ 63.5
Transfers between segments	11.6	2.8	—	(14.4)	—
Total	$ 62.0	$ 15.6	$ .3	$ (14.4)	$ 63.5
Total Revenues	$1,740.6	$290.1	$ 64.1	$(163.6)	$1,931.2
Income (loss) before extraordinary items - truck operations	$ (14.7)	$ 7.5	$ (4.4)	$ (0.2)	$ (11.8)
Income before extraordinary items - financial and leasing subsidiaries	13.5	3.2	—	—	16.7
Income (loss) before extraordinary items	$ (1.2)	$ 10.7	$ (4.4)	$ (0.2)	$ 4.9
Identifiable assets at December 31, 1987:					
Truck Operations	$ 724.0	$ 75.8	$48.6	$ (8.1)	$ 840.3
Financial and Leasing Subsidiaries	515.6	126.2	2.6	—	644.4
Total	$1,239.6	$202.0	$ 51.2	$ (8.1)	$1,484.7

Identifiable assets are those assets that are directly identified with the operations in each segment. Export sales included in United States sales totaled approximately $72,114,000 in 1989, $98,889,000 in 1988, and $82,605,000 in 1987.

Exhibit A–19

15. Stock Options, Awards, and Performance Units

The Company's 1988 Executive Long-Term Incentive Plan (the "1988 ELTIP"), which became effective on January 1, 1988, provides for the granting of awards, either in the form of stock options or performance units, to selected employees. An aggregate of 1,000,000 shares of authorized and unissued or treasury common stock is available for awards granted under the 1988 ELTIP.

Stock options granted under the 1988 ELTIP generally vest 25% on the first, 25% on the second and 50% on the third anniversaries of the awards and are exercisable at the fair market price of the Company's common stock on the date of grant. Subject to earlier termination, such stock options expire not later than ten years after the date of grant.

Awards of 14,825 performance units were granted in 1989 for the three-year performance period 1989 through 1991, with a value ranging from zero to a maximum of $150 per unit, payable in 1992. No performance unit awards were granted covering the 1990 through 1992 three-year period.

Prior to January 1, 1988, stock options and restricted unit awards were granted under the Company's 1983 Stock Option and Award Plan (the "1983 Plan"). The 1983 Plan was terminated as of January 1, 1988, except for options and awards which were previously granted to eligible employees.

The following table summarizes stock option and restricted unit award activity under the 1988 ELTIP and the 1983 Plan for the years ended December 31, 1989, 1988, and 1987:

	Number of Shares	Price Per Share
Outstanding December 31, 1988	**348,176**	$ 9.81—$21.88
Exercised or Paid	**(64,844)**	$ 9.81—$21.88
Granted	**629,500**	$ 5.88—$14.25
Cancelled	**(52,071)**	$10.88—$15.33
Outstanding December 31, 1989	**860,761**	$ 5.88—$21.88

	Number of Shares	Price Per Share
Outstanding December 31, 1987	391,689	$ 7.25—$21.88
Exercised or Paid	(93,013)	$ 7.25—$21.88
Granted	88,000	$11.88
Cancelled	(38,500)	$10.88—$21.88
Outstanding December 31, 1988	348,176	$ 9.81—$21.88

	Number of Shares	Price Per Share
Outstanding December 31, 1986	532,732	$ 5.65—$21.88
Exercised or Paid	(147,105)	$ 5.65—$21.88
Granted	33,600	$11.88
Cancelled	(27,538)	$10.88—$21.88
Outstanding December 31, 1987	391,689	$ 7.25—$21.88

As of December 31, 1989, options for 88,728 shares of common stock are exercisable and the remainder become exercisable through 1999. Restricted unit awards granted in 1987 vest over a two-year period; all other restricted unit awards vest over a five-year period.

Exhibit A–20

Mack Trucks, Inc.
and Consolidated Subsidiaries

NOTES TO CONSOLIDATED FINANCIAL
STATEMENTS

**16. Earnings (Loss)
Per Common Share**

The computations of primary earnings (loss) per common and common equivalent share are based on the weighted average number of common and common equivalent shares outstanding during the periods.

The computations of earnings (loss) per common share assuming full dilution were identical to the respective computations of primary earnings per common and common equivalent share. Information supporting the computations of earnings (loss) per common and common equivalent share for the years ended December 31, is as follows:

Number of Shares Used	1989	1988	1987
		in thousands	
Primary:			
Common stock outstanding at December 31	29,653	29,577	29,518
Common stock equivalents and weighting effect	58	82	693
Weighted average shares for primary earnings (loss) per common share computation	29,711	29,659	30,211

Earnings (Loss) Used	1989	1988	1987
		in thousands	
Primary:			
Income (loss) before extraordinary items	$(185,656)	$24,941	$ 4,924
Extraordinary items	237	6,845	(834)
Net income (loss) available to common shareholders	$(185,419)	$ 31,786	$ 4,090

Exhibit A–21

17. Quarterly
Financial Information
(Unaudited)

	Three Months Ended			
	March 31	June 30	Sept. 30	Dec. 31
	in millions, except per share data			
1989:				
Total revenues	$ 517.5	$ 545.3	$ 394.0	$ 401.0
Total costs and expenses	$ 513.9	$ 563.2	$ 483.2	$ 482.6
Income (loss) before extraordinary item	$ .7	$ (19.9)	$ (87.6)	$ (78.8)
Extraordinary item	.5	.3	.1	(.7)
Net income (loss)	$ 1.2	$ (19.6)	$ (87.5)	$ (79.5)
Earnings (loss) per common and common equivalent share:				
Primary				
Income (loss) before extraordinary item	$ 0.02	$ (0.67)	$ (2.94)	$ (2.65)
Extraordinary item	0.02	0.01	—	(0.02)
Net income (loss)	$ 0.04	$ (0.66)	$ (2.94)	$ (2.67)
Assuming full dilution				
Income (loss) before extraordinary item	$ 0.02	$ (0.67)	$ (2.94)	$ (2.65)
Extraordinary item	0.02	0.01	—	(0.02)
Net income (loss)	$ 0.04	$ (0.66)	$ (2.94)	$ (2.67)

	Three Months Ended			
	March 31	June 30	Sept. 30	Dec. 31
	in millions, except per share data			
1988:				
Total revenues	$ 504.0	$ 591.4	$ 523.5	$ 569.1
Total costs and expenses	$ 494.9	$ 579.5	$ 518.7	$ 550.2
Income before extraordinary item	$ 4.6	$ 7.9	$ 2.1	$ 10.4
Extraordinary item	.5	2.2	.7	3.4
Net income	$ 5.1	$ 10.1	$ 2.8	$ 13.8
Earnings per common and common equivalent share:				
Primary				
Income before extraordinary item	$ 0.15	$ 0.27	$ 0.07	$ 0.35
Extraordinary item	0.02	0.07	0.02	0.12
Net income	$ 0.17	$ 0.34	$ 0.09	$ 0.47
Assuming full dilution				
Income before extraordinary item	$ 0.15	$ 0.27	$ 0.07	$ 0.35
Extraordinary item	0.02	0.07	0.02	0.12
Net income	$ 0.17	$ 0.34	$ 0.09	$ 0.47

Net sales of heavy-duty and medium-duty trucks for the fourth quarter of 1989 totalled $370.8 million, 32% lower than 1988 fourth quarter sales of $544.7 million. Heavy-duty and medium-duty truck deliveries declined by 38% and 48%, respectively, compared to the 1988 fourth quarter, primarily due to the industry-wide decline in the North American truck market.

Cost of sales, as a percent of net sales, increased from 90.9% in the fourth quarter of 1988 to 108.2% in 1989, primarily caused by higher levels of fixed costs resulting from lower capacity utilization and higher warranty and related costs. Fourth quarter 1989 cost of sales was also adversely impacted by a $12.9 million settlement of disputed claims with a major supplier and a $12.3 million provision for termination and restructuring costs (see Note 12). Fourth quarter 1989 total costs and expenses also reflect a 97.9% increase in interest expense from the comparable 1988 period as a result of a higher average level of borrowings for both the parent company and financial subsidiaries.

Exhibit A–22

NOTES TO CONSOLIDATED FINANCIAL STATEMENTS

18. Subsequent Events

On February 16, 1990, the Company announced that a collective bargaining agreement with its Winnsboro, South Carolina employees represented by the United Auto Workers of America (UAW) was ratified by the employees and approved by the Company's Board of Directors. The labor agreement provides for the inclusion of the Winnsboro facility under the Master Agreement between the Company and the UAW, and for initial wage and benefit increases effective January 1, 1990. Other economic and benefit provisions are to be phased in over the term of the agreement, which expires in October 1992.

On February 15, 1990, the Company entered into an agreement in principle with RVI, under which, subject to certain conditions (including execution of the Credit Agreement below and satisfactory renegotiations of bank credit agreements of certain of the Company's subsidiaries), RVI will purchase $50 million of the Company's 8% convertible subordinated debentures having a term of 20 years. The debentures may be converted at any time into 7,009,550 shares of the Company's common stock and include antidilution provisions. If the debenture is converted, RVI would own 55.1% of the Company's common stock.

In March 1990, the Company and all its U.S. bank lenders have reached an agreement on the principal terms of a three-year syndicated secured credit agreement (the "Credit Agreement") under which the Company's bank borrowings of $143,250,000 would be consolidated into a three-year term facility bearing interest at 1.5% above the agent bank's alternate base rate and with amortization beginning after 18 months. The Credit Agreement includes a $5 million letter of credit facility and will also permit the Company to establish a revolving credit facility in a maximum amount of $50 million. The Company's ability to borrow under the revolving credit facility would depend on the levels of the borrowing base (as defined in the agreement) and the amount of debt or equity issued by the Company after the Credit Agreement's effective date. Security for the Credit Agreement would include the Company's inventory and the shares of stock of certain subsidiaries. While the Company does not expect that on the Credit Agreement's effective date any lenders will have agreed to provide credit under the revolving credit facility, the Company intends to seek institutions to provide such credit. The Credit Agreement contains covenants relating to, among other things, maintenance of a specified current ratio, and the sum of the Company's cumulative net income (loss) plus the proceeds of any future issue of subordinated debt or equity by the Company. Under the Credit Agreement, the Company would not be permitted to pay any dividends (other than stock dividends) on its common stock. Execution of the Credit Agreement is subject to agreement on final documentation and the purchase of $50 million of subordinated debt by RVI.

On February 23, 1990, Renault and AB Volvo announced their intention to exchange the shares and voting rights of forty-five percent of their respective truck and bus operations and twenty to twenty-five percent of their respective car operations. According to an RVI press release, the agreement is subject to approval by the Boards of the two companies, shareholders' committees and completion of a variety of governmental, social and administrative requirements. The Company does not anticipate any short-term impact and is unable to predict any long-term impact on its structure or operations as a result of the proposed agreement.

APPENDIX 2 FINANCIAL STATEMENT INTER-RELATIONSHIPS

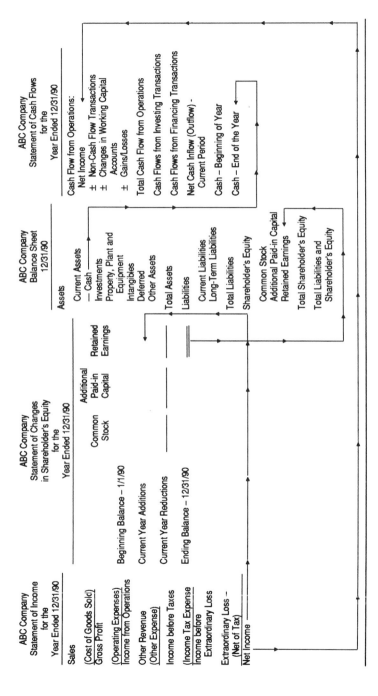

ABC Company Statement of Income for the Year Ended 12/31/90

Sales
(Cost of Goods Sold)
Gross Profit
(Operating Expenses)
Income from Operations
Other Revenue
(Other Expense)
Income before Taxes
(Income Tax Expense)
Income before Extraordinary Loss
Extraordinary Loss – (Net of Tax)
Net Income

ABC Company Statement of Changes in Shareholder's Equity for the Year Ended 12/31/90

	Common Stock	Additional Paid-in Capital	Retained Earnings
Beginning Balance – 1/1/90			
Current Year Additions			
Current Year Reductions			
Ending Balance – 12/31/90			

ABC Company Balance Sheet 12/31/90

Assets

Current Assets
 – Cash
Investments
Property, Plant and Equipment
Intangibles
Deferred
Other Assets
Total Assets

Liabilities
Current Liabilities
Long-Term Liabilities
Total Liabilities

Shareholder's Equity
Common Stock
Additional Paid-in Capital
Retained Earnings
Total Shareholder's Equity
Total Liabilities and Shareholder's Equity

ABC Company Statement of Cash Flows for the Year Ended 12/31/90

Cash Flow from Operations:
Net Income
± Non-Cash Flow Transactions
± Changes in Working Capital Accounts
± Gains/Losses
Total Cash Flow from Operations
Cash Flows from Investing Transactions
Cash Flows from Financing Transactions
Net Cash Inflow (Outflow) - Current Period
Cash – Beginning of Year
Cash – End of the Year

FINANCIAL STATEMENT CLASSIFICATION OF ACCOUNTS

Assets

Accounts Receivable
Advances to Affiliates
Advances to Employees
Bond-Sinking Fund
Building
Cash
Copyright
Deferred Taxes
Deferred Plant Reorganization
  Costs
Equipment
Franchise
Furniture and Fixtures
Goodwill
Idle Plant and Equipment
Income Tax Receivable
Intangibles
Interest Receivable
Inventory
Investment
Land
Leasehold Improvements
Loans Receivable
Marketable Securities
Notes Receivable
Organization Costs
Patent
Prepaid Insurance
Prepaid Rent
Stock Subscriptions Receivable
  Supplies

Vehicles

Liabilities

Accounts Payable
Accrued Compensation
Accrued Liabilities
Advances from Customers
Bonds Payable
Deferred Taxes
Dividends Payable
Interest Payable
Lease Payable
Mortgage Payable
Notes Payable
Pension (Obligations) Payable
Salaries Payable
Taxes Payable
Unearned Revenue

Shareholder's Equity

Additional Paid-In Capital
Foreign Currency Translation
Adjustment
Preference Stock
Preferred Stock
Retained Earnings
Treasury Stock
Unrealized Loss

Revenue

Dividend Revenue

Gain on Disposals
interest Revenue
Investment Revenue
Rental Revenue
Sales

Expense

Administrative Expense
Advertising Expense
Amortization Expense
Bad Debt Expense
Cost of Goods Sold
Depletion Expense

Depreciation Expense
Distribution Expense
General Expense
Income Tax Expense
Loss on Disposals
Payroll Expense
Payroll Tax Expense
Pension Expense
Promotion Expense
Property Tax Expense
Salary Expense
Selling Expense
Supplies Expense
Utility Expense

FINANCIAL STATEMENT
ACCOUNTS (ALPHABETIZED)

Account	Classification
Accounts Receivable	Asset
Accounts Payable	Liability
Accrued Liabilities	Liability
Accrued Compensation	Liability
Additional Paid-In Capital	Shareholder's Equity
Administrative Expense	Expense
Advances from Customers	Liability
Advances to Employees	Asset
Advances to Affiliates	Asset
Advertising Expense	Expense
Amortization Expense	Expense
Bad Debt Expense	Expense
Bonds Payable	Liability
Bond-Sinking Fund	Asset
Building	Asset
Cash	Asset
Copyright	Asset
Cost of Goods Sold	Expense
Deferred Taxes	Asset or Liability
Deferred Plant Reorganization Costs	Asset
Depletion Expense	Expense
Depreciation Expense	Expense
Distribution Expense	Expense
Dividend Revenue	Revenue
Dividends Payable	Liability
Equipment	Asset
Foreign Currency Translation Adjustment	Shareholder's Equity
Franchise	Asset
Furniture and Fixtures	Asset
Gain on Disposals	Revenue
General Expense	Expense
Goodwill	Asset
Idle Plant and Equipment	Asset

Income Tax Expense	Expense
Income Tax Receivable	Asset
Intangibles	Asset
Interest Revenue	Revenue
Interest Receivable	Asset
Interest Payable	Liability
Inventory	Asset
Investment Revenue	Revenue
Investment	Asset
Land	Asset
Lease Payable	Liability
Leasehold Improvements	Asset
Loans Receivable	Asset
Loss on Disposals	Expense
Marketable Securities	Asset
Mortgage Payable	Liability
Notes Receivable	Asset
Notes Payable	Liability
Organization Costs	Asset
Patent	Asset
Payroll Expense	Expense
Payroll Tax Expense	Expense
Pension (Obligations) Payable	Liability
Pension Expense	Expense
Preference Stock	Shareholder's Equity
Preferred Stock	Shareholder's Equity
Prepaid Rent	Asset
Prepaid Insurance	Asset
Promotion Expense	Expense
Property Tax Expense	Expense
Rental Revenue	Revenue
Retained Earnings	Shareholder's Equity
Salaries Payable	Liability
Salary Expense	Expense
Sales	Revenue
Selling Expense	Expense
Stock Subscriptions Receivable	Asset
Supplies	Asset
Supplies Expense	Expense
Taxes Payable	Liability
Treasury Stock	Shareholder's Equity
Unearned Revenue	Liability
Unrealized Loss	Shareholder's Equity
Utility Expense	Expense
Vehicles	Asset

LIQUIDITY, PROFITABILITY, OPERATING AND LEVERAGE RATIOS

Liquidity Ratios

Ratio	Calculation
Current ratio	$\dfrac{\text{current assets}}{\text{current liabilities}}$
Quick ratio or acid test ratio	$\dfrac{\text{cash + marketable securities + receivables}}{\text{current liabilities}}$
Working capital	current assets - current liabilities

Profitability Ratios

Ratio	Calculations
Gross profit percentage	$\dfrac{\text{gross profit}}{\text{net sales}}$
Cost of goods sold	$\dfrac{\text{cost of goods sold}}{\text{net sales}}$
Operating expense percentage	$\dfrac{\text{total operating expenses}}{\text{net sales}}$
Income from operations percentage	$\dfrac{\text{income from operations}}{\text{net sales}}$
Income before tax percentage	$\dfrac{\text{income before taxes}}{\text{net sales}}$

Net income percentage	$\dfrac{\text{net income}}{\text{net sales}}$
Earnings per share	$\dfrac{\text{earnings available to common}}{\text{weighted average common shares}}$
Return on equity	$\dfrac{\text{net income}}{\text{stockholders equity}}$
Return on assets	$\dfrac{\text{net income}}{\text{total assets}}$
DuPont Analysis of return on equity	net income percentage × asset turnover × leverage

Operating ratios

Ratio	Calculation
Accounts Receivable:	
Turnover	$\dfrac{\text{credit sales for the period}}{\text{accounts receivable}}$
Collection period	$\dfrac{\text{number of days in the period}}{\text{accounts receivable turnover}}$
Accounts Payable:	
Turnover	$\dfrac{\text{purchases for the period}}{\text{accounts payable}}$
Days outstanding	$\dfrac{\text{number of days in the period}}{\text{accounts payable turnover}}$
Inventory:	
Turnover	$\dfrac{\text{cost of goods sold}}{\text{inventory}}$

| Days in inventory | $\dfrac{\text{number of days in the period}}{\text{inventory turnover}}$ |
| **Assets Turnover:** | $\dfrac{\text{net sales}}{\text{total assets}}$ |

Capital Structure or Leverage Ratios

Ratio	**Calculation**
Current debt to equity	$\dfrac{\text{current liabilities}}{\text{stockholder's equity}}$
Long-term debt to equity	$\dfrac{\text{long term debt}}{\text{stockholder's equity}}$
Debt to equity	$\dfrac{\text{total debt}}{\text{stockholder's equity}}$
Times interest earned	$\dfrac{\text{net income before taxes and interest}}{\text{stockholder's equity}}$

Selected Reading List

Financial Statement Analysis: A Practitioner's Guide
Fridson, Martin S.
Wiley, 1991

Financial Statement Analysis: A Strategic Perspective
Stickney, Clyde P.
Harcourt Brace Jovanovich, 1990

Financial Statement Analysis: Using Financial Accounting Information
Gibson, Charles H.
PWS-Kent, 1989

Financial Statement Analysis: Theory, Application, and Interpretation
Bernstein, Leopold A.
Irwin 1988

Financial Statement Analysis
Woelfel, Charles J.
Probus Publishing Co., 1988

Fundamental Analysis
Ritchie, John C., Jr.
Probus Publishing Co., 1989

Intermediate Accounting
Kieso, Donald and Weygandt, Jerry J.
Wiley, 1987

INDEX

A

Accelerated Cost Recovery System (ACRS), 34
Accounting
    full disclosure, 1
    Principles Board (APB)
        Opinion #15, 28
        Opinion #18, 17
        view of policies, 74
Accounting Trends and Techniques, 44
Accounts receivable ratios, 91, 93-94
Acid test ratio, 91, 93
Almanac of Business and Financial Ratios (The), 89
Almanac of Business and Industrial Financial Ratios (The), 89
American Institute of Certified Public Accountants (AICPA), 44
Analysis of financial statement *see* Ratio Analysis
    benefits/limitations, 87
    data base, 88
    definition, 86
    procedure, 90
Annual report, 8
Assets turnover ratio, 102, 105

B

Balance sheet
    assets, 1, 13
    cash and cash equivalents, 14
    inventory, 15
    receivables, 15
    basics, 11
    data limitations, 22
    equity, 1, 21
    fixed assets, 17
    liabilities, 1, 18
    long-term assets
        goodwill, 18
        intangibles, 17
        investments, 16
        property, plant and equipment, 17
    preparation, 12

C

Capital
    additional paid-in, 64
Changes in business ownership, 75
Collection period ratio, 91, 93-94
Common-size statements, 88
Common stock, 61
Common stock equivalent (CSE), 38
Contingent liabilities, 83
Cost of goods sold percentage ratio, 102-104
Current debt to equity ratio, 106-107
Current ratio, 91-92

ABOUT THE AUTHOR

Professor Rose Marie L. Bukics joined the Lafayette College Faculty in 1980 after serving as an auditor for the "Big 8" firm of Deloitte and Touche and as an internal auditor for a large public utility. She was promoted to associate professor in 1988 and was also the recipient of the oustanding teaching award in 1988. A native of Scranton, Pennsylvania, Professor Bukics is a Summa Cum Laude graduate of the University of Scranton and Lehigh University. She is also a certified public accountant (CPA) in the state of Pennsylvania. Professor Bukics previously published *The Handbook of Credit and Accounts Receivable Management* with co-author Walter Loven (Probus, 1987). Her professional affiliations include the American Institute of Certified Public Accountants, the Pennsylvania Institute of Certified Public Accountants and the American Accounting Association.

Exceptional Titles from the Investor's Quick Reference Series

Mutual Funds Explained: The Basics & Beyond,
Robert C. Upton Jr., $12.95

Wall Street Words: The Basics & Beyond,
Richard J. Maturi, $12.95

Forthcoming Titles . . .

Managing Your Investments, Your Savings & Your Credit: The Basics & Beyond,
Esme E. Faerber, $12.95, Available in October 1991

How Wall Street Works: The Basics & Beyond,
David L. Scott, $12.95, Available in February 1992

ORDER FORM

Quantity	Title	Price

Payment: MasterCard/Visa/American Express accepted. When ordering by credit card your account will not be billed until the book is shipped. You may also reserve your order by phone or by mailing this order form. When ordering by check or money order, you will be invoiced upon publication. Upon receipt of your payment, the book will be shipped. Please add $3.50 for postage and handling for the first book and $1.00 for each additional copy.

Subtotal	
IL residents add 7% tax	
Shipping and Handling	
Total	

Credit Card # _____

Expiration Date _____

Name _____

Address _____

City, State, Zip _____

Telephone _____

Signature _____

Mail Orders to:

PROBUS PUBLISHING COMPANY
1925 N. Clybourn Avenue
Chicago, IL 60614

or Call:

1-800 PROBUS-1